YOUR MONEY
Personality

YOUR MONEY Personality

UNLOCK THE SECRET TO A RICH AND HAPPY LIFE

Liz Koh

AWA PRESS

First edition published in 2008 by Awa Press, 16 Walter Street, Wellington, New Zealand.

National Library of New Zealand Cataloguing-in-Publication Data
Koh, Liz, 1955-
Your money personality : unlock the secret to a rich and happy life / Liz Koh.
Includes index.
ISBN 978-0-9582629-1-0
1. Money—Psychological aspects. 2. Finance, Personal—New Zealand. I. Title.
332.4019—dc 22

Designed by Liane Design, Wellington
Typeset by Jill Livestre, Archetype, Wellington
Author photograph by John Nicholson
Printed by McPherson's Printing Group, Australia
This book is typeset in New Century School Book

www.awapress.com

To Anita, Tara and Marisha, my three beautiful daughters, who have been my motivation and my joy. Thank you for the sacrifices you have made so that I can fulfil my dreams.

Contents

Before we start... 1

Money and personality 7

How to discover your money personality 13
- Are you a hoarder? 15
- Are you an achiever? 17
- Are you an entrepreneur? 19
- Are you a thrill-seeker? 21

Where does your money personality come from? 23
- Your beliefs about money 24
- Respect for money 30
- Stage in life 34
- Perception of wealth, and of how wealthy you are 43
- Financial experiences 45
- Motivation 48

Make the most of your money personality 51
- Modifying your money personality 57

You and your partner 65
- Working together 71
- The power of difference 71

The six easy steps to create wealth 73

Step 1 – Take stock of your potential 75
- Money personality 76
- Net financial assets 76
- Where is your money going? 84

Step 2 – Work out what money can do for you 87
What is the role of money in my life? 88
How much money do I really need? 89

Step 3 – Decide how much wealth you want to create 93
The compulsory goal – emergency funds 94
Working-life goals and retirement goals 95
Putting it all together 107
Being realistic 109

Step 4 – Find ways to create wealth 111
Cut costs and save without sacrificing your lifestyle 112
Create more net income 126
Use technology to create wealth automatically 134
Multiply your money 150
Protect your nest egg 189

Step 5 – Record your wealth-creation plan 201
Your plan and your money personality 202
How to write your plan 203

Step 6 – Make it happen 207
How to improve your chance of success 208
Setbacks 210
Start creating wealth today! 217

Where to invest your money 219
Managed funds 220
Direct investments 233

How to protect your money 261
Insurance 262
Family trusts 267
Asset-splitting and testamentary trusts 272

Choosing and working with a financial adviser 275
Finding a good adviser 276
What service will be provided? 277

Further reading 279

Index 282

Before we start…

IF YOU HAVE PURCHASED THIS BOOK, OR EVEN BORROWED it from a friend, congratulations! You are clearly a person who wants to maximise your money, live life to the full, and not just dream dreams but *make them come true*. The good news is, you're already halfway there. By learning to understand your money personality, and following my advice about how to manage and invest your money, you will be amazed at what you can achieve. This book's not pie-in-the-sky – it's based on my years of experience helping clients realise their dreams. **People just like you.**

This book can't change your life – only you can do that – but it can get you started on a whole new way of looking at money that will increase your wealth dramatically, and take away much of the stress and anxiety many of us experience in dealing with our personal finances.

Right now you may be thinking that the amount of wealth you will create in your life will be based on how hard you work, or how much money you start out with. This is, of course, partly true. But what really counts – and can make you a winner – is your attitude towards money and how keen you are to 'play the game'. I call this your money personality, and in years of advising people how to maximise their money I have come to realise it is the single most important factor in wealth creation.

Many books on wealth creation have been written and read. Some people buy numerous books and attend numerous seminars, yet the books and seminars make no lasting impact on their ability to create wealth. That's because they fail to take account of the vital role their individual money personality plays in the wealth-creation process.

Your money personality is the result of a number of things:

The lessons you have learned about money from other people, especially your parents and other close family members.

Your experiences with money, both as a child and an adult.

Your stage of life.

Understanding your money personality is the key to understanding not only how you can make more money, but how you can take better control of it – and, most important of all, enjoy it more.

In this book, money and wealth are treated not as ends in themselves, but as the means to ends – the way to fulfil our life goals.

Many of us go through life feeling constrained by money. Why? After all, we work hard to get it. It should enable us to live the life we want, rather than setting limits on what we can do.

A few years ago I had as a client a recently retired, very successful businessman. George had emigrated to New Zealand from Europe when he was around 20 with little more than a few coins in his pocket. Through hard work and shrewdness, he had achieved his lifetime goal of acquiring ten million dollars in assets. On his retirement, he had cashed up his business, bought a nice new house and put around nine million dollars in the bank.

So he was brilliantly set up, right? Wrong. Having worked so hard to build up his assets, George was fearful of losing any of his money. The frugal habits that had helped him create his wealth were preventing him from spending it. After two years in retirement, he still had no idea what he wanted to do with his money. In fact, it had become a huge problem to him. He knew that putting it in the bank was safe but he also knew it would give him a low return. However, he didn't know what else to do.

So how successful was George really? He had been so focused on money as an end in itself that he had neglected to derive the full benefit of his wealth. There was now a real danger that his life would end before he was able to do so.

An obvious first step for George was to think about what benefits he wanted to receive from his money. What purpose could it serve in his life?

Being clear about the purpose of money in your life won't just help clarify what to do with it once you have it: it will also give you the motivation to manage your money better and do things differently.

And if you want to change your life, you need to change your actions.

> **If you do what you have always done, you will get what you have always got.**

CASE STUDY

Helen and John came to see me because they were struggling to keep up with their financial commitments, despite having a combined income of around $150,000. These commitments included a large mortgage on a house in a top suburb, private school fees for two children, annual overseas holidays and a lavish weekly food budget. In short, they were living beyond their means.

Despite having been married 15 years, Helen and John still managed their money separately, and as a result neither took overall responsibility for their financial affairs.

It was clear from talking to them that they had very different money personalities. John had a conservative approach. He was uncomfortable with having a large mortgage and felt the couple's priority should be to reduce their debt. He didn't feel the need to live in luxury, but wanted to live a simple life with few possessions, no debt, and enough income to enable him to develop his writing talents by working only four days a week.

Helen, on the other hand, wanted her children to be able to experience the best that life could offer – an excellent education, a large, comfortable family home in a prestigious neighbourhood, and regular overseas travel. Her own parents had struggled financially and she was determined that her children would not suffer the hardship she had as a child. Helen's view was that it was all right to keep increasing the mortgage if the money was being used to give the children a better life.

The tension between John and Helen was immense. Without making drastic changes, they would have continued on through life, constantly arguing and struggling to make ends meet. Instead they set up a new structure for their bank accounts, agreed on a budget, and prioritised what they wanted to spend their money on.

The key was, first, learning to understand and accept each other's attitudes to money and figuring out how conflicts could be resolved; second, establishing clear financial goals and a plan to achieve them; and, third, taking action to make the necessary changes.

This book will give you the tools to do what Helen and John have done. You will learn how to be smarter with your money, and make the best use of the financial resources you have in order to achieve your life vision. You will discover the things in life that are important to you, and devise strategies to achieve them. And if you have a partner whose attitude to money is different from yours, you will find ways of working together more positively and successfully.

Remember, the more you want out of life the more focused you will need to be, the more changes you will need to make, and the more risks you will need to take. Perhaps you just want to have enough money to retire on. Perhaps you want to be able to buy luxuries from time to time without worrying where the money will come from. Or perhaps you want to make a million dollars within the next ten years to achieve some really ambitious goals. Whatever your desires, this book will show you how to achieve them.

Before you begin, though, you need to commit to taking action and making whatever changes are necessary, starting from now.

So, are you ready?

Money and personality

IN MY CAREER AS A FINANCIAL ADVISER I HAVE MET PEOPLE from many different walks of life and in greatly varying financial circumstances. Some of my clients are extremely wealthy, while others struggle to live from one pay-day to the next. One thing I discovered early on was that the amount of wealth created by a client was not determined by how much money he or she had earned in their lifetime. In fact, some of my wealthiest retired clients had lived for most of their lives on modest incomes.

This got me thinking. If it wasn't income that determined wealth, what was it? Of course, for some people sheer good luck is a factor: there is the occasional lottery winner, or the person who has received a large inheritance. But it soon became clear to me that, for most people, psychological factors determined how much wealth they had.

Take Shirley and Robert for instance. A professional couple in their early fifties, they have a debt-free house and a substantial investment portfolio for their retirement. In recent years, some of their wealth has been used for overseas travel and assisting their children with education costs.

What has driven Shirley and Robert to get to their present comfortable position? Both have a strong need for security and an aversion to debt. When the couple bought their first house they set themselves the goal of repaying the mortgage as soon as possible. As the family grew, they purchased a bigger house and took out another mortgage. Once again, this was repaid as quickly as possible. However, the couple still worry about whether they will have enough money for later in life, when they will be retiring or working less.

Another of my clients, Jan, has a different view of money and security. Jan came to see me several years ago after receiving a large divorce settlement from her husband. At the time, she was living in a modest home in one of the less affluent suburbs, and before the settlement she had been struggling financially.

In place of conserving and growing her new-found wealth, Jan decided to use it to buy a new home and financially support her children. Rather than being driven to accumulate wealth, she is driven by a desire to live in a pleasant environment and make other people happy. Although she is now less wealthy in dollar terms than she was at the time of her settlement, having spent most of the cash left over after buying the house, she is enjoying life and using her money to achieve the things in life that are important to her.

Not everybody achieves a happy outcome with their money, however. Judy is a real estate agent whose income fluctuates from month to month and year to year, depending on how the property market is faring. She is the sort of person who spends money when she gets it. Even though she knows that she needs to have money in reserve to help her through the times when the market is slow, she finds it impossible to have money without spending it. She celebrates a large commission payment by going on an overseas trip or buying jewellery, and in between house sales she has to increase her mortgage to pay her bills. Now she is in her fifties with a large mortgage, which will force her to either sell her house and buy a cheaper one, or keep working for many years to come.

Analysing the differences between my clients over the years has led me to the conclusion that two things most strongly reveal your money personality:

your level of desire to create wealth

your willingness to take risks.

Let's talk first about desire. If you don't have a strong desire to create wealth, it is unlikely you will do so. And a strong desire to create wealth goes hand-in-hand with having a clear life vision, so you will need that too. True wealth-creators are usually driven by something other than the creation of wealth as an end in itself. The motivating force may be a desire for power, success and status, or a desire to help other people.

To get motivated, you have to be really clear about what you stand to gain once you have succeeded. Your success will be determined by how clear and how ambitious your goals are, and how confident you are dealing with money.

People with a strong desire to create wealth feel they are able to influence the amount of money they attract into their life. They therefore actively look for opportunities to create wealth. They tend to have an optimistic view of life and believe they can overcome barriers. They put no limits on what they can achieve.

Let's stress again that it is not the *amount* of wealth you want to create that is critical, but the *strength of your desire* to create it. The two may not necessarily be related. Being successful doesn't always mean creating a lot of wealth. It means creating the amount of wealth you desire, however much that is.

To create more wealth, you need to take more risk.

The second revealing personality trait is your attitude to risk. Risk and return go together.

Whatever we do in life, we take risks. Even everyday activities such as hanging out the washing, driving to work, playing sport or crossing the road have elements of risk that, if you took the statistics seriously, would have you curled up in bed all day.

Fortunately, most people can see that the rewards of being able to enjoy a full and active life outweigh the risks involved, providing you are sensible and don't unwittingly or knowingly expose yourself to *too much risk*. The same principles apply to managing money.

To create significant wealth you need to understand and manage risk. A risk-averse person will usually monitor money carefully and worry about losing it. He or she will avoid debt if at all possible. Commonly they will not trust other people when it comes to money, and will keep their money in a safe place such as a bank account.

Of course, all of us are risk-averse at some stage in our lives. We are usually at our most risk-averse when we have the responsibilities of a family, and when we are on a low income, for example in retirement. Conversely, we are at our least risk-averse when we are:

- young, with no dependants, or
- middle-aged but not yet retired, and with no dependants. Our children, if we have them, are now leading independent lives.

Both of these are good times to focus on creating wealth.

To return to my clients Shirley and Robert, both have a strong desire to create wealth, driven by their mutual desire for security in retirement. They are not, however, willing to take a high level of risk to create that wealth; they prefer to get there by saving hard and investing with moderate risk.

Jan, on the other hand, has a low desire to create wealth. For her, having a nice home to live in and being able to support her children financially is much more important. Jan has a high tolerance for risk in that she is not especially concerned about her financial security, either now or in the future. Rather, she sees money as something that can satisfy her immediate, rather than long-term, needs.

After years of impulse spending, Judy is concerned about her future financial situation now that she is older, but because she finds it difficult to change her spending habits, it looks precarious.

These different attitudes are often ignored by financial planners and authors of books on how to get rich. They assume that everyone has the same approach to money. This is why so many people end up feeling frustrated: they can't seem to make any financial progress and so they frequently give up and revert to their old habits where money is concerned.

Once you understand your relationship with money, it's easy to know what changes you need to make to have a rich and happy life.

8

How to discover your money personality

PSYCHOLOGISTS HAVE DEVELOPED ALL SORTS OF TESTS and theories to categorise personalities. You may have heard of the Myers-Briggs Type Indicator and Friedman's Type A/ Type B theory. When it comes to the way people think about money, and what they do with it, I've found it's remarkably simple to figure out what sort of personality you have. My experience helping people manage their money and increase their wealth has shown me that there are just four basic types.

Here are the four money personalities:

The hoarder

The achiever

The entrepreneur

The thrill-seeker.

These personalities are defined by different levels of desire to create wealth and willingness to take risks. These are shown in the chart below. The vertical axis of the chart shows desire to create wealth; the horizontal axis shows willingness to take risks.

People who have a low desire to create wealth and a low willingness to take risks I classify as hoarders. Achievers also have a low willingness to take risks, but they have a high desire to create wealth. In the top right-hand corner, entrepreneurs have both a high desire to create wealth and a high willingness to take risks, while thrill-seekers have a low desire to create wealth and a high willingness to take risks.

The first step to wealth-creation is discovering which of these personalities you are. This will be the key to understanding what you do with money now – and how you can do things a whole lot better.

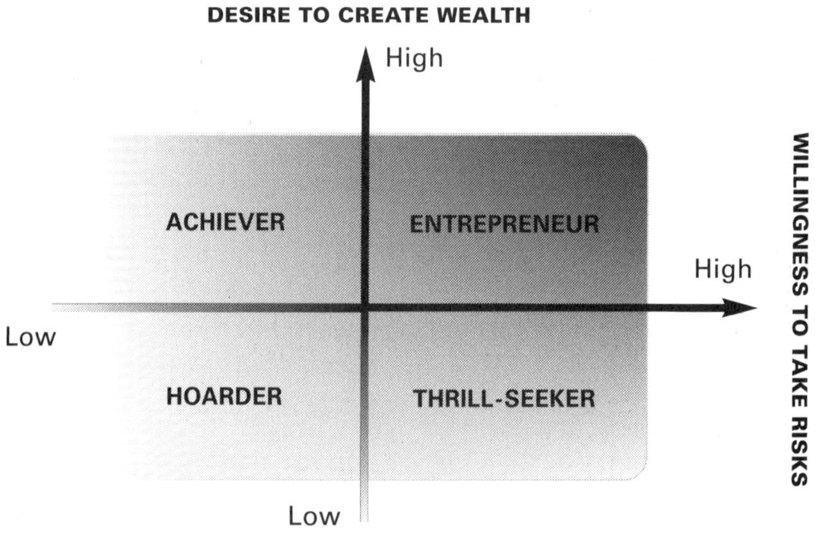

Are you a hoarder?

A hoarder is risk-averse, and has a low desire to create wealth. Hoarders will generally succeed in creating wealth only if they have substantial assets or high earning potential.

Typically, hoarders are careful, conservative money managers. They live by a strict budget and keep spending under tight control. They know how much money they have and where it all goes, and prefer to keep their money somewhere secure, such as in a bank account.

Hoarders dislike debt, and if they have a credit card they pay it off every month. When a hoarder wants to buy something he or she will save up, rather than using hire purchase or loans. They will take on debt only if they have to – for example, to buy a home.

Hoarders are typically content with their lot. They prefer to see their wealth grow slowly and steadily, rather than take risks with the possibility of large gains. As well as being cautious, they are also suspicious of others and prefer to look after their own affairs rather than seek advice.

If you are a hoarder, you will no doubt end up with a nice pile of cash in the bank, but being overcautious you will miss out on opportunities to make your money work better for you.

Your challenge is to get more confident about money.

- Learn as much as you can about investing and investments.
- Seek expert advice from a trustworthy person as to which investments are secure and which are not.
- Try stepping outside your comfort zone in a small way.

CASE STUDY

My clients Bert and Alice were a lovely couple in their eighties. Both had lived through hard times, and from an early age had learned to live within their means and save. Bert had had a good government job with an average salary; Alice had also worked in paid employment for a few years, before giving up her career to be a full-time mother.

Bert's goal throughout his life had been to make sure his family wanted for nothing, and he succeeded in achieving this. The couple came from an era when you didn't buy anything unless you had saved the money for it, but that didn't mean they went without. Bert used the wealth he created through saving and being debt-free (other than a small mortgage) to provide a good standard of living for his family, and after his retirement he and Alice travelled and enjoyed life. Both valued non-material things, and because their needs were simple they were easily met.

These two hoarders managed their money carefully and wisely, and although they never had a high income they amassed a small fortune. Bert took great pride in keeping records of his investments and carefully charted the growth in their value. When Bert and Alice passed away, they left a large inheritance for their two daughters, neither of whom had any idea that their parents were so wealthy.

CASE STUDY **HOARDER**

Are you an achiever?

If you are an achiever you will be relatively conservative, but your conservatism will be accompanied by a strong desire to succeed in life, and to create wealth. You will also be quite analytical and cautious in your approach to money.

Achievers are usually well-educated or well-read (or both), and have highly paid professional jobs and/or ambitious career plans.

Status-conscious, they will spend money on things that create an impression of affluence and success, such as a home in a high-priced suburb, an expensive car, private school education for their children, designer clothes, home improvements and overseas holidays. While their spending is high, it is usually on items that have a lasting value.

Sometimes an achiever will fall into bad habits, such as spending money they can't afford on others, feeling as though they have to live up to an image, or being embarrassed about people knowing their real financial circumstances.

> Your challenge is to look and feel affluent without spending all your money and increasing your level of debt.

- Rather than amassing a wardrobe full of designer clothes, buy a few high-quality items and mix them with cheaper ones.
- Instead of redecorating your whole house, do one or two rooms.
- If you are spending too much money eating in the best restaurants, sometimes visit them just for coffee and dessert instead.

CASE STUDY

My client James is an achiever in his late thirties. He has a high-paying job with an annual bonus, and his salary has increased every year for the last ten years. He and his partner have purchased a house with a sea view in a good area, and are hoping to be able eventually to re-sell it for a significant capital gain.

As James commutes to work, he feels he must have a late-model car for comfort and reliability. He has a young family, and feels that to give them the kind of childhood he would have liked he should provide the latest technology, such as a computer, video camera, DVD player and PlayStation. His annual bonuses are used to purchase such items. He hopes to take his family to Disneyland for a holiday and wants to start a saving fund with this in mind. However, he is struggling to find the money to do this.

Because James spends all he earns, the capital gain on his family home is presently his only way of creating wealth. A bit of a handyman, he spends his spare time making additions and alterations to the home, and these are financed by an ever-increasing mortgage. James's view is that the additional borrowing is not a problem as long as he can service it, as the house is going up in value by more than the amount being borrowed.

Are you an entrepreneur?

Entrepreneurs are the true creators of wealth, people prepared to take an initial high level of risk in the expectation of high returns. Entrepreneurs can succeed despite having few assets or a small income. If you are an entrepreneur you will not feel restricted by a lack of money. If you have no money of your own, you will use someone else's.

Money is what gives you choices in life and you use it to help you excel – for example, by embarking on a new venture such as setting up your own business, or undertaking further education or training. Your spending will, therefore, be on things that have the potential to produce a return, or add to your ability to create wealth. Unfortunately, however, you can fall into bad habits with money, so debts pile up and budgeting falls by the wayside. The fortunes of entrepreneurs can vary between extremes: you may be a millionaire one year and bankrupt the next.

Entrepreneurs typically seek out like-minded people to do business with, or seek advice from. To have credibility with an entrepreneur, you need to be an entrepreneur yourself as they see themselves as being different, even superior, to other people.

> Avoid losing everything by putting some of your acquired wealth into safe assets.

- Don't have all your assets tied up in one or two ventures; aim to diversify your assets.
- Make sure that you separate your personal and family assets from your business assets and protect them from creditors, for example by using a family trust.
- Always be aware of what the worst-case scenario may be if your venture struggles to succeed. Have a plan for knowing when to bail out and how to minimise your losses.

CASE STUDY

Richard, a self-made millionaire, is a typical entrepreneur. As soon as he turned 15, he left school, took up an apprenticeship as a painter, and spent his spare time building up his own painting business. As soon as his apprenticeship was completed, he worked full-time in this business.

From the age of 23 he started buying old rundown houses, doing them up and selling them for a large profit. He financed his first house by selling his car and borrowing money from a solicitor for six months. By the time the money was due to be repaid, he had renovated the house and sold it for a significant capital gain, allowing him to buy several more properties.

Thereafter followed many other ventures, some successful, some not – a pizza parlour, a gym, a private detective agency, a decorative concrete company. Fortunes were made, lost, and made again. When times were tough financially, he would simply go without, even at one stage resorting to eating offal he had cooked for his dog.

These days, Richard is a wealthy man, and has returned to his old trade of painting. His latest venture is to add to his wealth by franchising his business. What Richard lacks in education he makes up for in a strong desire and determination to create wealth, courage to take risks, and willingness to seek advice from like-minded people.

CASE STUDY **ENTREPRENEUR**

Are you a thrill-seeker?

Thrill-seekers are gamblers. They take risks for the sheer enjoyment of it, and would rather continue taking new risks than accumulate wealth. They often have a high level of income, which is used for short-term satisfaction. They live by the motto 'Easy come, easy go': money is to be spent here and now. Credit cards are used to their limits. Mortgages can be extended to pay for an overseas holiday.

If you're a thrill-seeker, a day out shopping and spending lots of money will give you a real buzz. Sometimes the purchases will be of unnecessary or even unwanted items, but the thrill makes it worthwhile. While achievers are also big spenders, they tend to spend money on things of lasting value, whereas thrill-seekers will spend money on just about anything that provides instant satisfaction.

Once the thrill of the purchase has worn off, a thrill-seeker will often feel remorseful about their actions and overwhelmed by their level of debt.

> Your challenge is to stop spending and start saving. Your spending should be done with money you have saved, rather than with money you have borrowed.

- Ensure you have strict controls on the amount of credit you can access.
- Set a budget that shows your income, saving and spending – and stick to it.
- Invest any long-term savings in places where you can't get your hands on the money in the short term.

CASE STUDY

Maxine is the kind of person with whom you immediately feel comfortable. Her pleasure in life comes from her ability to establish a close rapport with many different people, and to surround herself with attractive possessions and a beautiful garden. She has so many things of beauty in her home that there is very little room to spare, and a wardrobe bursting with so many clothes she could never possibly wear them all.

Money seems to run through Maxine's fingers. Although she is in her fifties, she still has a large mortgage on her house, as she has had to refinance her credit card several times when it has reached its limit.

Maxine does not have a desire to create wealth for the future: it is more important to her to enjoy life in the moment. She is not afraid of the future, believing that she will always find a way to survive, even if it means eventually selling her home and living in a small apartment.

Maxine is a thrill-seeker in that, for her, money is something that provides instant pleasure rather than long-term security. It will always be a struggle for her to find enough money to pay her bills, but she is one of the happiest, friendliest people you could meet, and has a wide circle of friends.

CASE STUDY **THRILL-SEEKER**

8

Where does your money personality come from?

BY NOW YOU WILL HAVE RECOGNISED YOURSELF – AND perhaps other people such as your partner and parents – in these profiles. Your money personality has been shaped by many different things.These often hidden attitudes are much more important to financial success than how much money you start out with and what your job is.

As I worked with clients from many different backgrounds and stages of life, I came to recognise strong personality patterns that affected their ability to both create and retain wealth.

The more I looked into this, the more I came to see that an individual's money personality is shaped by six factors:

Beliefs about money

Respect for money

Stage in life

Perception of wealth, and of how wealthy you are

Financial experiences

Motivation.

Your beliefs about money

Beliefs about money can strongly affect both your desire to create wealth and your willingness to take risks. These beliefs are often grounded in childhood and the messages you received then, and in what you have learnt as an adult from people you admire. Being aware of the influences that have helped shape your beliefs about money will help you develop a positive attitude towards money. You cannot attract money into your life if your beliefs about it are negative, or you feel you don't deserve to have it. Fears and phobias about money can also reduce your willingness to take risks.

What money is...

The way we treat money is often rooted in our childhood and the things our parents taught us. Listed below are common sayings I remember from my own childhood. You may find it enlightening to make your own list.

Money is the root of all evil.

Money doesn't grow on trees.

There is no such thing as a free lunch.

Time is money.

Money makes the world go around.

Money can't buy you love.

Money can't buy you happiness.

The best things in life are free.

You can't have everything.

A fool and his money are soon parted.

It's my money, and I'll do what I want with it.

Love doesn't pay the bills.

Let the buyer beware.

Put your money where your mouth is.

You get what you pay for.

A penny saved is a penny earned.

Penny-wise, pound-foolish

If wishes were horses, beggars would ride.

The rich get richer, the poor get poorer.

You have to have money to make money.

And what we should do with it...

Save for a rainy day.

Look after the pennies and the pounds will take care of themselves.

Waste not, want not.

Neither a borrower nor a lender be.

Don't marry for money, but marry where the money is.

Don't throw good money after bad.

Don't let your money burn a hole in your pocket.

Don't bet what you can't afford to lose.

Don't flash your cash.

Don't bite off more than you can chew.

Have sayings like these influenced your behaviour or beliefs about money?

CASE STUDY

An inability to save can sometimes be traced back to a feeling that money is evil. Keith was brought up with this idea.

He came to see me for the first time when he had paid off the mortgage on his house and wanted to start saving for his retirement. Keith's family had to work hard to survive, and were exploited by people with money. Accordingly, Keith had grown up thinking that wealthy people were nasty people. It was almost as though they were the enemy, and becoming like them would be disloyal to his family.

Keith's career path has taken him into jobs that he enjoys doing and which fit his cultural values. Often, these have been lowly paid positions that have given him a good deal of personal satisfaction. However, as Keith has chosen not to focus on money, he has struggled to build up his retirement fund. Whenever it has built up he has withdrawn the funds to help his children or people less fortunate than himself. It's as if his subconscious fears about money are compelling him not to accumulate it.

Keith has adopted the view that if he looks after his children now, they will look after him in the future – almost as if the financial resources of the whole family unit will be shared over time according to need. I only hope he is right!

CASE STUDY **BELIEFS ABOUT MONEY**

Money fears

Childhood experiences can result in our having fears and anxieties about money. Do any of these apply to you?

I am afraid I will not be able to keep up my mortgage payments.

I am scared of making a mistake with my money and losing everything I have.

I am worried about paying for my children's education.

I am afraid I will never be able to pay off my credit card debt.

I am afraid I'll lose my job and not be able to pay my bills.

I am afraid of not having enough money to live on when I retire.

I am afraid of what other people think about how much I earn and how much I have saved.

I am worried about how I am going to pay next month's bills.

Worrying about money not only stops us from developing our full potential, but can promote a vicious circle of unhappiness and feeling deprived.

> You need to feel positive about money to attract it into your life.

Fears and anxieties about money are endemic among hoarders, who are generally pessimists. When dealing with money they will quickly pick out all the things that may go wrong, and conveniently ignore all the things that may go right.

Hoarding is driven by fear – fear that there will never be enough money, that jobs may be lost, that illness or death may occur, that there will be a global economic meltdown. If you are a hoarder, the root of these fears may be in your childhood, traumatic experiences and/or lack of knowledge. You will need to understand where your fears and anxieties come from so you can overcome them, and thereby increase your willingness to take risk and create wealth.

CASE STUDY

Marion came to see me for some retirement planning advice. Her parents had always struggled financially, and from an early age Marion believed she had no choice but to follow the same route. She had assumed that she would never have a brilliant career, had to take whatever life dished out to her, and had little control over her future.

As a result, she had put self-imposed barriers around what she could achieve – almost as if to step outside those barriers would be to break the laws of the universe that had predetermined her destiny.

Marion's passive approach to life had left her with a lowly paid job that she disliked, a house in a poor suburb, and no partner or children. In her late fifties, she was getting by through being frugal. She had paid off her mortgage and was now saving for her retirement, still with the expectation that she would never have a large amount of money to provide for her needs.

Marion's pessimistic view was holding her back from growing her wealth in the last decade before her retirement. However, Marion was not an unhappy person. She had accepted her lot and felt she was managing her money well. If only she could see what she could have achieved had she stretched her boundaries – even a little.

CASE STUDY **BELIEFS ABOUT MONEY**

The Depression factor

If your parents or grandparents lived through the 1930s' Depression, there's a good chance that some of their beliefs about money have been passed down to you. The maxims 'waste not, want not' and 'penny-wise, pound-foolish' were typical of the era.

Most people who lived through this time became skilled at making their money go further, and afterwards became very good savers. However, they were too afraid to risk money on speculative ventures.

It has been found time and time again that people who are successful wealth-creators share certain beliefs and attitudes.

- They feel positive about money, and are confident dealing with it.
- They believe they are able to influence the amount of money they have in their life.
- They are not afraid to take calculated risks.
- They believe they are in control of their money, rather than their money (or lack of it) being in control of them.
- They believe money is a means to an end, rather than an end in itself.
- They are willing to work hard, but believe that hard work in itself is not the best or only way to make money.
- They treat money with respect.

Respect for money

If you want your money to work well for you, it's a good idea to treat it with respect. Be careful and responsible with it, keep track of it, don't waste it or lose it unnecessarily, and *think about it in a positive way*.

Over the years my clients have made many interesting throwaway remarks about money that have proved to be important in analysing why they have money problems.

Where does money go?

I spend more than I can afford on birthday and Christmas presents.

I spend more money on my friends than I can afford.

I sometimes buy clothes, realise I have made a mistake, but don't bother to return or exchange them.

When I shop I buy my favourite brands of food and drink, rather than the brands that are on special.

I often buy takeaway food or eat out because I can't be bothered cooking.

I hardly ever pay my bills on time.

I often withdraw extra cash when I use Eftpos to make a purchase.

If I have cash in my wallet, I spend it.

I don't bother shopping around for cheaper prices – it's easier to just buy it as soon as I find it.

Sometimes I buy new things for my house when the old one was really still okay.

How many of these apply to you?

HOARDERS AND MONEY

Of all the money personality types, hoarders have perhaps the greatest respect for money.

Hoarders fear losing their money and so they look after it carefully, spending it only after considering whether their purchase is affordable, and good value.

Don't go shopping with a hoarder unless you have a lot of time to spare while he or she looks for bargains. I have a good friend who is a hoarder. He takes twice as long to buy his groceries as I do. He will purchase the cheapest brand of every item on his list, even if he saves only a few cents. To him, those few cents saved have a high value when added together.

In extreme cases, a hoarder's respect for money can be so great that accumulating money becomes an end in itself. Think Scrooge McDuck, with his stockpiles of gold coins. Having too much respect for money (to the point where it is revered) is just as unhealthy as having no respect at all.

ACHIEVERS AND MONEY

Achievers also respect money, but with an element of greed.

To an achiever, money represents success, status, and the ability to enjoy a comfortable, even luxurious, lifestyle. Whereas a hoarder will accumulate money and keep it safe, an achiever will accumulate money to spend on things he or she values.

At the extreme, an achiever's lust for money can be insatiable. The more money he or she has, the more they spend, and the more they need to maintain their lifestyle. This attitude has come to be seen as typifying Generation Y – the generation who want a wealthy lifestyle now, even though they can't afford it.

A healthy respect for money means valuing it – but in moderation. If you are an achiever, don't let your need for money rule your life.

ENTREPRENEURS AND MONEY

For an entrepreneur, money is a commodity or a resource that can be used to create a business or an opportunity.

It is a necessity, but has no intrinsic value. If some of it is lost along the way, that's just part of the price of eventual success. Entrepreneurs don't respect money any more than they respect any other resource they need to achieve their higher purpose – whether time, materials or technology.

While no one likes to fail, a true entrepreneur sees failure as a stepping stone to eventual success, and therefore is usually philosophical about losing money. In the extreme, entrepreneurs can be so indifferent towards loss that their actions affect not only themselves but others who are associated with, or dependent on, them.

Their selfishness or lack of concern for others is evident with the collapse of high-profile companies where entrepreneurs have taken huge risks, not only with their own money but with other people's money as well. While entrepreneurs may have the skills to rebuild their fortune, this is not necessarily so for the others involved. If you are an entrepreneur, learn to respect money sufficiently that you don't take too much risk with it, especially when other people could be affected by your actions.

THRILL-SEEKERS AND MONEY

The ultimate downfall of thrill-seekers is their disrespect for money.

To put it bluntly, if you are a thrill-seeker, you are careless with money. It's as if money falls from the skies: it has no value until it has been converted into something that gives you instant satisfaction.

Underneath that disrespect is often an emotional need of some kind. Some thrill-seekers are addicted to spending: they get an emotional high from it. This is no different from the high that overweight people get when they tuck into a favourite snack, or gamblers get when they hit the jackpot.

To find out whether you are addicted to spending, think about how you feel immediately before, during and after spending money. If you're a spending addict, you will tremble with anticipation as you line up a purchase. It's as though you are *compelled* to make the purchase. You will say things like 'I *have* to have those shoes.' If the shoes aren't available in the right size, you will feel as if there's been a huge disaster.

Thrill-seekers are, in fact, experts at inventing reasons for buying something, and the likely terrible consequences if they don't.

> **'If I don't buy that dress, I'll have nothing to wear to the office party next week.'**
>
> **'That plasma TV is such a bargain – it will never be available at that price again and I would be crazy not to buy it now.'**

During the purchase itself, a spending addict feels an incredible sense of happiness, even euphoria. Typically, however, once this has worn off remorse sets in. The remorse may not be immediate. It may even come weeks later. The dress that was once a must-have hangs unworn in the wardrobe because it doesn't fit quite right. All the faults that were overlooked in the euphoric moment of purchase now seem overwhelming.

If you think you may be a spending addict, it could be helpful to seek counselling to understand the emotional needs you are trying to meet through your spending, and to find other ways of meeting those emotional needs.

Of course, disrespect for money isn't necessarily linked to a spending addiction. It may be that you are simply careless with money. You leave it lying around your house in a multitude of places, rather than keeping it safely in one place. You don't keep good records of how much money you have and where it all goes. Your money disappears in dribs and drabs – mostly on food and drink, entertainment, magazines and other small stuff.

People with these habits often come from a family background where money flows freely. This doesn't necessarily imply wealth, just a way of life where spending takes priority over saving.

The task for thrill-seekers is to learn to respect money by taking care of it and not wasting it.

Stage in life

Your money personality evolves with you over your lifetime. Events, experiences and the situations in which you find yourself all help shape the way you use money and relate to it.

Broadly speaking, there are six stages of life. All will impact on your attitude towards risk and wealth-creation.

Stage 1 – Young and free

What's happening?

Life is all about fun and discovering the world. There is plenty of time to do everything in life you want to do. You have few responsibilities, and your income is increasing from one year to the next as your career develops. If you happen to lose or spend all your savings, you have plenty of time to save up again.

You and money

You are most able to take risks at this stage of life, as you are keen to experiment and have time to recover if things go wrong. However, you are limited by lack of knowledge and experience. Mistakes can easily be made.

What you need to know

It is vital to learn how to manage debt, especially in a society where credit is freely available. Getting into debt early in life can have disastrous and long-lasting consequences. This is a real danger for thrill-seekers and entrepreneurs in particular.

Stage 2 – Settling down

What's happening?

You may be in a long-term relationship, and considering having children. If so, your dilemma will be working out what is the best time to sacrifice income and incur more expense in order to start your family.

Before you take this step, your focus is likely to be on lifestyle spending (house, car, travel) as you seek to create a comfortable environment for your future family, and get the travel bug out of your system.

If and when you do take on family and career responsibilities, you will become more aware of safeguarding the people who depend on you.

You and money

A house, a mortgage and lower household income go along with a new family. It's a struggle to make ends meet. This is generally a time of financial survival rather than wealth-creation.

What you need to know

Thrill-seekers and achievers who are in nest-building mode should be wary of spending too much on lifestyle assets, and taking on a big mortgage, which will impose a heavy financial burden. This could cause conflict with entrepreneur and hoarder partners, who are customarily less inclined to spend money this way.

Stage 3 – Expanding horizons

What's happening?

Your income is on the way up again as the children go off to school and your career takes off. A bigger house and a new car may be top of your priority list. This means a bigger mortgage and higher expenses.

You and money

As your disposable income increases, your money personality will determine whether you spend it or invest it.

Differences in money personalities between partners will come to the fore, and you will need to find ways of resolving them. Achievers and thrill-seekers, if not kept in check by entrepreneurs and hoarders, may use growing incomes to spend more rather than save more. Entrepreneurs could go charging ahead of hoarders at an alarming rate, putting entrepreneur–hoarder relationships under great pressure.

Finding time to manage your financial affairs will be critical as you are pulled in all directions – career, family, and what's left of your social life. It's likely your money will end up having to look after itself.

What you need to know

Lack of attention to your financial affairs during this phase will see much of your income being used ineffectively. This is the crucial time to get your life and your money on track. If you head off in the wrong direction, you will find it hard to recover during the next phase.

Stage 4 – Consolidating assets

What's happening?

Income is still increasing, and you and your partner may now both be working full-time. The mortgage is under control, but the teenagers aren't! Time for fun again as you have spare money for things you couldn't afford before, such as going out for dinner, taking the children on an overseas holiday, and upgrading the family car.

You and money

This can be a time of conflicting needs and priorities. You may have a strong desire to create wealth, yet you are less willing to take risks than when you started your career. You may need to save more so you can build up wealth, but your expenses are high, making saving difficult, if not impossible. And your personal needs and desires may be in conflict with those of your partner and dependants.

On top of this, you feel as though you are beginning to run out of time to make changes to your life. You may have a strong desire to change your career or set up your own business, but feel burdened by your high level of outgoings and therefore not willing to face a potential drop in income. Is it any wonder that this stage of life often culminates in mid-life crisis?

What you need to know

If you haven't resolved the money personality differences between you and your partner by now, there is a good chance they will begin to have a negative impact on your relationship. It's vital you sort out a way forward that will work for both of you.

Stage 5 – Peaking

What's happening?

You're at the peak of your career. Unfortunately this also means your income is at its peak and probably starting to decline. You worry about having enough money for retirement. You also worry that you may die before you get to enjoy your retirement. Hoarders and achievers will be concerned with preservation and lifestyle, while entrepreneurs and thrill-seekers may want a last-ditch effort at making money and living it up before retirement.

You and money

There is a conflict between spending money so as to enjoy life while you are relatively young and healthy, and saving for retirement. Your mortgage is all but gone and you've begun accumulating a retirement nest egg. You don't want to lose what you have – most of which is the equity in your home – but you want to use what you have to create even more. You are looking for a high level of return on your investments but without a high level of risk – if only there were such a thing!

What you need to know

This is your last chance to save for your retirement. Whatever you have at the end of this stage is largely what you will have available for the rest of your life. As you get closer to this point you will have to reduce your spending to a level that will match the income you will have available when you ease back on work or retire. It's not easy to cut back on spending, but if you don't there is a real risk that in the first year or two of retirement you will be dipping into your savings more than you had planned to do.

Stage 6 – Enjoying the fruits

What's happening?

At this stage you are reaping the returns of your younger days. Wealth-preservation, rather than wealth-creation, is important. The major issue is how to spread out your money to cover a secure and comfortable old age. This means finding the right balance between keeping risks low, while at the same time growing wealth sufficiently to keep ahead of inflation and sustain a pleasant lifestyle.

It can be quite a dilemma knowing whether to spend most of your retirement capital in the early years, when you may be best able to enjoy it – for example buying a new car and going on overseas trips – or whether to leave enough of a buffer so that you never have to worry about money.

And then there is the issue of inheritance. Nowadays, many people feel that leaving a large inheritance for their family is not a priority: if there's anything left for them, it's a bonus. Others feel they would like to give them a helping hand for the future.

You and money

Your situation in this stage of life will be largely determined by how well you have managed your money in your working life. If you've done well and have a large investment portfolio, you can afford to be less risk-averse than if you have meagre savings.

Most, although not all, retirees and people lessening their workload become hoarders. Entrenched thrill-seekers may continue to follow their instincts, but eventually they run out of money and are forced into being hoarders just to survive. Retired entrepreneurs are usually happy to cash up their riskier ventures and take on a more conservative achiever- or even hoarder-like approach.

Achievers have spent their lifetime accumulating lifestyle assets, and retreat willingly into hoarderdom.

What you need to know

Your biggest risk during this stage is not losing your money, but running out of money before you run out of time. Investing your money too conservatively may mean that your returns are not enough to keep ahead of inflation and tax, and your standard of living will drop over time. Using up your capital too soon on things like new cars and overseas travel can lead to money worries later.

Have a backup plan in place, such as an agreement with your children about how they can help you financially, or investigate home equity release through one of the many schemes that are now available.

These schemes allow you to free up capital you have in your home without having to make repayments in your lifetime. Interest on the loan is compounded, and the full amount owed is repaid when the home is sold. While the beneficiaries of your estate will receive less than the sale value of your house, you will have had the opportunity to enjoy a worry-free retirement.

Attitudes towards inheritances have changed in recent times. Many children do not expect to receive a large inheritance, nor do parents have a desire to leave one. For older people with no other option available, home equity release through a reputable company can be the difference between misery and happiness.

Each stage of life has parallels with a money personality.

Stage 1 is the thrill-seeker phase: it's all about being young, adventurous and mostly broke.

Things get more serious in stages 2 and 3. This is when the achiever personality dominates: life is all about accumulating lifestyle assets and proving to the world that you are a success.

In stages 4 and 5, as the children get older and the need for wealth-creation for your old age becomes more urgent, you may become more entrepreneurial. With a solid financial base, you can now take a few more risks in order to increase returns.

Stage 6 is about being a hoarder, preserving wealth, income and lifestyle.

This is not to say that everyone under the age of 30 is a thrill-seeker, and everyone over the age of 65 is a hoarder. It simply means that, whatever your dominant money personality, at different stages of life you will be pulled more towards an approach to money that suits that particular stage.

For example, a hoarder will be slightly more willing to take risks in stage 1, and more keen to do whatever is necessary to create wealth in stages 4 and 5. A thrill-seeker may only become really aware of the need to create wealth by stage 5, by which time panic about retirement will have probably set in.

CASE STUDY

My client Jonathan is a good example of an investor who is influenced by perceptions of wealth and future earning potential. Jonathan is 30, single and an artist. Art is his passion, and he is one of those artists who paint what they want to paint, rather than what will sell. His art is not easily understood by others.

Jonathan's art is so important to him that he has no plans at this stage to have a family, as this would put financial pressure on him to the extent that he might have to seek employment and give up painting full-time. Fortunately, however, a close relative has recently left him a substantial amount of money, enough to buy a house and provide a modest income for the rest of his life.

Although Jonathan could use this money to make even more money, he is quite content with his lot. He has more money now than he could ever have dreamed of having through his own endeavours. He lives frugally – his main expense is his painting materials – and expects to have meagre earnings from sales of his paintings. His goal is to eventually become recognised as a significant artist.

Because Jonathan considers himself wealthy already and expects his future earnings to be low, he has a low desire to create wealth and a low willingness to take risks. Jonathan is a hoarder.

CASE STUDY **PERCEPTION OF WEALTH**

Perception of wealth, and of how wealthy you are

Not everyone defines wealth in monetary terms. For some of us, being 'wealthy' simply means having a comfortable house to live in and food in the refrigerator. For others, it means being financially free, with no debts, and with sufficient passive income to be able to choose not to work. Still others want enough money to buy expensive goods and live a jetsetter lifestyle.

As I talked about earlier, attitudes and expectations you formed in your childhood may have a strong influence on how you perceive wealth. You may have grown up believing you are destined never to be wealthy and must accept whatever life dishes out to you, and that any attempt to achieve more will be doomed to failure. Or you may be the complete opposite – self-confident, optimistic, and determined to succeed despite the odds.

Your attitudes and expectations can become a self-fulfilling prophecy. Believing you will never be wealthy will cause you to act in a certain way, and your negative attitude will mean that any steps you take to create wealth will probably fail. This, in turn, will reinforce your belief that you are destined never to be wealthy.

Your attitude towards wealth-creation will also be influenced to some extent by your current financial situation and your future earning potential.

Your current financial situation

If you see yourself as already wealthy, you may be less inclined to want to create more wealth. However, feeling financially secure may make you more willing to take risks.

Conversely, if you see yourself as lacking in wealth, you may have a strong desire to create wealth, but also an aversion to risk: you won't want to chance losing the little you have.

CASE STUDY

Anna is a reformed alcoholic. She spent many years as a single parent, living on a benefit and spending more than she should on alcohol. There were times when there wasn't enough money to buy food.

After nearly 20 years without touching the bottle and now in her late fifties, Anna finally has a well-paying job. However, she finds herself unable to manage her money effectively: she is held back by her belief that she is destined for a life of poverty. Spending a few dollars on a luxury such as a manicure is enough to keep her awake at night with remorse, even though she can now afford it.

Anna finds it difficult to imagine accumulating money, and is, therefore, unable to set goals for herself. How can she have a goal that she believes will be impossible to achieve? She is entrenched in a mindset of living from one day to the next, and manages her money accordingly. That means she is constantly checking the balance in her account and worrying about whether she is going to have enough to pay all her expenses and to acquire enough possessions to enjoy a comfortable life. While she has a small amount of savings, her negative mindset almost seems to attract situations that mean that she has to dip into her nest egg on a regular basis, so it doesn't grow.

CASE STUDY **PERCEPTION OF WEALTH**

Your future earning potential

Your perceptions about your future earning potential can also influence your approach to money. If you think your future earnings will be *high*, you may be more willing to take risks, on the assumption that losses, if any, can be made up from future income.

If you think your future earnings will be *low* – for example, because you have been made redundant or are close to retirement – your willingness to take risks will also be low.

Although such conditioning is powerful, there is always a large element of choice in how you react to the circumstances you find yourself in. You can choose to take a passive approach, and accept the barriers and limitations you perceive to exist. Or you can choose to be proactive, and find ways around them.

> Visualise yourself as a successful, wealthy person. This will help you succeed in reaching your goals.

Financial experiences

Past experience, or lack of experience, with money can also have a profound effect on your money personality. Hoarders, for example, often admit they are cautious because they don't have enough knowledge or experience of money to be able to do anything differently.

People who leave financial affairs to their partner can fall into this category when the partner leaves or dies. This used to be particularly the case for women, but fortunately there is a growing trend for women to take responsibility for their financial affairs, managing their own income and spending, and/or managing joint finances.

Having a bad experience with money can cause even a natural entrepreneur to be cautious. If, for example, you have made a bad investment based on too little or incorrect information, you won't trust similar investments in the future.

Property investment is a good example. First-time property investors are susceptible to purchasing properties that make good family homes, but produce a poor return on investment when rented out. Combine a low investment yield with a poorly selected tenant who trashes the property and you have a quick sale of the property, and an investor who says, 'Residential property as an investment? You must be joking. Never again!' Yet had the investor approached the purchase armed with more knowledge and experience, the outcome may have been entirely different.

Other people's experiences can also have an impact. Your parents or friends may have had an investment go bad, and you have sworn not to make the same mistake. Or you may have read a news story about people losing their shirt in shares, property or finance companies and thanked the heavens it wasn't you. Experience of past global recessions can also influence behaviour. Fear the world may have another economic meltdown has engendered many a hoarder.

The sharemarket crash of 2002–2003 rekindled such fears. Many investors who had made the mistake of buying shares at their peak, panicked and sold them when the market fell, thus crystallising their losses. Reports of people having their retirement funds cut in half frightened others watching on the sidelines – even though the losses had come about through irrational decisions. Investors who had made rational decisions based on knowledge and experience, either reducing their investments at the top of the market or riding out the fall, didn't make the headlines.

The more you understand the markets in which you are investing, and the more experience you have, the easier it will be for you to create wealth. It pays to start learning how to manage your money early in life.

> The earlier you start managing money, the more confident you will be, and the more able to create wealth.

CASE STUDY

Ross and Margaret are a couple in their sixties who have both had successful careers. Throughout their married life they have managed their money separately. Each month Margaret pays half their joint expenses to Ross, who then pays the bills.

They also have separate arrangements for long-term saving and this has worked well: each has had to take responsibility for saving, and for keeping day-to-day finances under control.

This is an unusual situation for a couple of this era. It wasn't so long ago that it was commonly believed that the man should look after financial affairs, while the woman's role was to spend the housekeeping allowance. The result now is that many retired widows find managing their investments difficult and stressful.

This couple is different. Margaret has invested her savings over many years without discussing her affairs with Ross. In fact, he had no idea that she had accumulated such a tidy sum. By investing separately, Ross and Margaret were able to place their money in investments that suited their individual preferences, and retain a feeling of financial independence.

Now they have reached retirement age, Ross and Margaret have combined their savings to make a healthy nest egg that will provide them with a comfortable lifestyle. And both are capable of being solely responsible for their investments when the other dies.

CASE STUDY **FINANCIAL EXPERIENCES**

Motivation

At the most basic level, we are motivated by only two things – a desire to gain pleasure and a desire to avoid pain. Achievers gain pleasure through status symbols and a comfortable lifestyle. Entrepreneurs gain pleasure from success, and thrill-seekers find spending money satisfying and pleasurable. Hoarders, on the other hand, are often motivated by fear, and wish to avoid the pain of being financially insecure or suffering financial loss.

How motivated are you to create wealth? If you want it really badly, you will be motivated to achieve it. And the more wealth you want to create, the more motivation you will need.

To be highly motivated, you have to be very clear about what you want and the benefits you stand to gain. There's no point creating wealth for its own sake: it has to be the key to getting what you want out of life – whether this is security, freedom, independence, the ability to help your family or other people, or anything else that's important to you.

Achievers and entrepreneurs, the people with the strongest desire to create wealth, are very clear what they want out of life, and as a result are driven and focused.

> If you are not clear what you want out of life, you won't succeed.

Successful people know that nothing equips you better for success than a positive mental attitude – taking an optimistic view of the world where you see opportunities rather than threats, and strengths rather than weaknesses.

The ability to visualise a successful outcome is another attribute that is common among successful people. If you really hanker for a holiday on a tropical island, visualising yourself on that holiday is a powerful way of motivating yourself to achieve it. Imagine getting on the plane, arriving at your destination to a warm welcome, lying in a deck chair beside the pool, walking on the beach, feeling the gentle tropical breeze on your face.

Naturally, there will be times when you feel less motivated, or lose focus because of things that are going on in your life. When this happens it is important to consciously make time to reflect on your priorities and get motivated again. It helps to share your goals with a partner, friend or adviser who can help you stay on track.

CASE STUDY

When I set up my business as a financial adviser, I planned to build a successful business within twelve months. I had a strong vision of creating something from nothing, and putting all my knowledge and skills to the test while focussing on the things I am most passionate about – people and money.

Many things didn't go according to plan. It took much longer to build my client base than I had expected, international share markets lost value in four consecutive years, causing fear and panic among investors, and the company to which I was franchised went crashing down in flames. There were times when I wanted to give up and return to a corporate life with a regular income.

To help me get through this period, I surrounded myself with people who were setting up businesses themselves, or were in well-established businesses that they had created. Developing close relationships with these people showed me that what I was experiencing was no worse than what most entrepreneurs faced. All I had to do was to stick with it and find ways around the obstacles. My support network and my clear sense of purpose gave me the energy and confidence to keep going.

CASE STUDY **MOTIVATION**

8

Make the most of your money personality

LIFE IS NEVER BLACK AND WHITE AND WE ALL HAVE AN element of each money personality type. Even the most conservative hoarder will occasionally splash out on an extravagant purchase, and a thrill-seeker will sometimes manage to hoard money – if only for a short time. However, your money personality will be dominated by one (or occasionally two) of the main types. Once you understand your money personality and where it's come from, you have the power to make some changes.

While you can't change your money personality completely, you may be able to adopt beneficial behaviours from other personality types.

TIPS FOR **HOARDERS**

You have good money habits. You live well within your means, are good at budgeting, and always know exactly how much money you have in the bank. However, you tend to be overly cautious with money and suspicious of advice from others. As a result, your investment portfolio will probably comprise a narrow range of low-yielding investments.

In the extreme, hoarders can be so concerned about saving, and so fearful of one day running out of money, that they don't get as much enjoyment out of life as they should. Perhaps some time in the past you have had a bad experience with money, or perhaps your parents lived through bad times and passed on their money fears to you. Try and take an objective approach, rather than allowing irrational fear to dictate.

1. Overcome investment caution by reading and talking to others about how best to handle your financial affairs. Gaining more knowledge will give you confidence to open up a wider range of investment options, with potentially higher returns than you are getting at present.
2. Make the most of your good money habits by regularly putting money into a savings account or investment that will give you a good return.
3. Calculate how much money you need to save for your retirement, and in addition set aside some money for an emergency fund.
4. Review your insurance cover to take care of any potential financial risks through death or illness.
5. Once you have catered for these needs, any surplus funds can be spent on enjoying life. Loosen up a little.

CASE STUDY

Jill came to see me after she received a large settlement from her former husband. During the protracted negotiations she had lived a frugal existence as a single mother, eking out a strict budget with not a dollar to spare.

Then her life changed. As well as receiving the settlement – a large lump sum – she now had a new partner who was well off. Jill almost had to pinch herself to believe that she had choices about how to use her money. For the first time, she could choose whether to spend or save.

Because she had struggled for so long, Jill's natural inclination was to continue to save every spare dollar she had, as she couldn't believe her bad times were really over. Once I showed her that, with her current level of savings, she was well on track to achieving her retirement objectives, she was able to consider using some of her lump sum to improve her quality of life. She bought new clothes, had her broken teeth fixed and took a short overseas trip.

Although a long-time hoarder, she adopted some behaviours of an achiever. She gradually let go of the reins on her money and learnt to find the right balance between spending for enjoyment now and saving for security in the future.

TIPS FOR **ACHIEVERS**

You are hard-working, determined to succeed in life, and want nothing but the best for your family. The problem for some of you is that the lifestyle you strive for is beyond your present income. You are a couple of steps ahead of yourself: you've spent your annual bonus before you've received it, and the salary increase you're expecting to get in a few months has already been worked into your household budget.

You believe the only way you can get ahead is to work harder. You feel as though you're on a treadmill that's going faster and faster. You need to find a way of slowing down.

1. Take a break from spending: learn to save first and then spend, rather than buying on credit and then having to work harder to pay off the debts.

2. Try and find ways of making more money that don't require a lot of extra effort – for example, by finding a higher-paying job or taking in a boarder.

3. Find ways of giving your family a good life that doesn't rely so heavily on material possessions or spending a lot of money. A family picnic at the park can be just as much (or more) fun than a meal out at a café or fast-food restaurant. Spending time doing things with your children will often make them happier than receiving the latest toys or electronic equipment.

4. Let go of the belief that good quality and high price are inseparable. Seek advice from hoarder friends who shop around for the best deals. Whether it's clothes, furniture, sports equipment, hardware or anything else, use the 'mix and match' principle: buy a few good quality items and mix them with lower priced items.

5. Finally, stop thinking that other people will measure your success by your material possessions. Why should you keep striving in order to please somebody else? *Live your life for you.*

TIPS FOR **ENTREPRENEURS**

You are true wealth-creators, but you have probably lost almost as many fortunes as you have made. At times your willingness to take a punt can be your downfall. It can also cause problems with people in your life. Because you are prepared to make sacrifices in your present living conditions to invest for the future, your partner and family can feel deprived – and extremely anxious at the level of risk you are taking. I have seen instances where entrepreneurs have dealt with this by entering into ventures without their partner's knowledge, on the grounds that if they don't know about it they won't worry. The result is often a broken relationship.

As a successful entrepreneur, you won't trust the advice of other people unless they have proved themselves by being successful. Success in your terms is not related to academic background, but to their attributes and acquisitions, and how much wealth they have created.

Your two biggest challenges are retaining the wealth you create and maintaining good relationships with family, friends and colleagues.

1. Be clear about what is 'safe' money and what is 'play' money, even keeping them in separate ownership structures such as family trusts and companies. Use some of the safe money for home comforts for the other people in your life.

2. Surround yourself, both personally and professionally, with people who can keep track of your financial situation and ensure you have put in place checks and balances to reduce some of the risk you face.

3. Use these ways to reduce or limit risk.
   - Establish trusts and limited liability companies.
   - Ensure you fully research new business ventures, and undertake proper due diligence on businesses you are thinking of buying.
   - Put in place systems to monitor and forecast your cash flow and expected returns.
   - Bring in other partners to share the risk and contribute skills.
   - Get advice from accountants, lawyers, professional mentors or coaches, and hire employees with good administrative abilities.
   - Take out insurance.

4. With each successful venture, put some funds into a safe investment for the future – don't gamble everything you have on a new venture.
5. Reduce your life partner's potential anxiety by keeping him or her fully informed of what you are doing, the potential risks and returns, and how you intend to keep the level of risk to an acceptable level.

TIPS FOR **THRILL-SEEKERS**

You love spending and so your money is often frittered away on things that don't give you lasting pleasure, or that you never really needed in the first place. Your starting point is to learn to respect money. This means going back to the basics.

1. Take stock of your financial situation: what is your net worth and how is it changing from one year to the next? Are you going backwards financially by getting deeper into debt? Are you just managing to make ends meet? Or are you able to save a little every year?
2. Have a look at your bank and credit-card statements for the last three to six months and categorise each item. You probably already know what you are guilty of spending too much money on, but it will be a good reality check to quantify it.
3. Next, set yourself a budget. Rather than getting into too much detail trying to add up how much money you need for every item, set some broad categories for spending. The sections later in this book on budgeting and establishing money-management systems will be important for you.
4. Try some goal-setting. The best way to shift your thinking from short-term, or even instant, gratification is to have clear long-term goals you are passionate about. Leave constant reminders of these goals around your house and workplace, and in your wallet or purse. Perhaps you have always wanted an overseas holiday, a new car or some new furniture.

5 Once you've identified your long-term goals, start saving. If you are a real novice, start with something you can save for in a few months. Even small successes can give a huge boost to your confidence in your ability to save. Over time, set more ambitious targets.

6 Share your goals with friends who can help keep you on target, and discourage you from squandering your savings before you have reached your goal.

Modifying your money personality

Looking at the diagram again, you can see that modifying your money personality will mean modifying either your desire to create wealth, your willingness to take risk, or both – depending where you are starting from and where you want to end up.

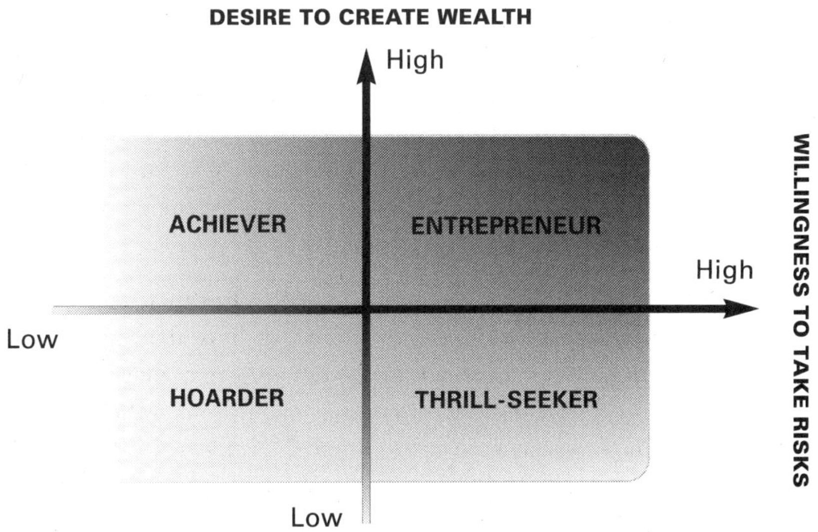

It is obviously going to be a lot easier to change one aspect than both. If, for example, you are a hoarder, becoming more entrepreneurial will mean increasing both your desire to create wealth *and* your willingness to take risk. However, if you are an achiever who wants to be more entrepreneurial, you will have to increase only your willingness to take risk.

It may be that you wish to reduce your desire to create wealth – for example, to move from being an entrepreneur to being more of a hoarder. Or you may wish to be less willing to take on risk – for example, by becoming less of a thrill-seeker and more of a hoarder.

It is not impossible to acquire new behaviours around money, but it does require commitment and a good understanding of why you are the way you are. Perhaps your aversion to risk stems from a bad experience with an investment or business venture? You will need to regain confidence in your ability to find good business or investment opportunities. That may mean seeking advice from an expert, or doing more research on opportunities before you invest money in them.

At the other end of the spectrum, you may be an impulsive thrill-seeker who wants to take fewer risks. A good start would be to delay major purchase and investment decisions for a week while you seek advice from someone with more of an analytical approach.

> Think about the money personality traits you would ideally like to have. Which of your current behaviours and attributes would you like more of? Which would you like less of?

CASE STUDY

I was approached for advice by Marcus, a young man in his early twenties who had decided that he wanted to make a million dollars by the time he was 30. He had just moved into the area and had a promising new job, albeit on a low salary. He was hoping that in his spare time he could set up a business that would provide a passive income and make his fortune. He wanted to know how he could raise enough money to get this business off the ground.

On interviewing Marcus at his workplace, I discovered that when he had moved to the area he had visited one of the local stores and bought about $3000 worth of appliances for his flat on hire purchase. He had also taken out a $15,000 loan to buy a flash car. While I was there, the woman who delivered lunches to his workplace popped in and reminded him that he owed her $20 for his lunches that week.

The young man who aspired to being an entrepreneur was really a thrill-seeker in disguise. I told him that to make his fortune he would need to change his behaviour to leave behind some of his thrill-seeker habits. In his situation, a true entrepreneur would have bought second-hand appliances and a push bike and made his own lunches, so as to have enough money to invest in his business venture.

CASE STUDY **THRILL-SEEKER**

It is difficult to change your money personality drastically in a short space of time, but it *is* possible to adopt wealth-creation strategies that use the positive aspects of your personality and minimise the negative aspects.

I've talked about six things that influence money personality:

Your beliefs about money

Your respect for money

Your stage in life

Your perception of wealth, and of how wealthy you are

Your financial experiences

Your motivation.

To find ways of introducing new behaviours, make a list of all the influences and experiences that have contributed to your money personality under each of these headings.

Now, brainstorm some ideas about actions you could take to counteract the negative influences. There is nothing you can do about your stage in life (unless you have discovered the secret of turning back the clock), but there are ways you can work on the rest.

Simply being *aware* of the contributing factors can often lead to a change, but there are practical steps you can take as well.

Let's look at some examples.

Beliefs about money

Take Anna, the reformed alcoholic, who believes she can't save money and is destined to a life of poverty (see Case study, page 44).

Anna simply needs some facts about her true financial situation. By analysing her income and her expenses she will see that she can, in fact, save. Once she has set aside the savings she needs to make for her medium- and long-term needs, she can spend whatever is left on a manicure or some other treat without feeling guilty.

Respect for money

Creating respect for money is all about getting into good money habits. One useful technique is to make a list of good habits that you promise to practise, and leave it somewhere you will see it every day.

Things that may appear on your list:

I will pay my bills on or before their due date.

I will spend less than I earn.

I will save before I spend.

I will pay off my credit card every month.

I will set a limit on the dollar value for each gift I buy.

I will buy the best value for money.

It's not easy to change habits, so don't try and change too many at once. Set a goal for each habit you are trying to change, and reward yourself when you achieve the goal. For example, you may aim to pay your bills on time for the next six months. When you achieve it, you will buy yourself a CD.

Perception of wealth, and of how wealthy you are

It's often difficult to judge how your wealth compares with others you consider to be your peers, especially as, in many cultures, money and wealth are not discussed openly. A good way to start is to make a list of all your assets and liabilities. The difference between the two is your net worth – in other words, the amount of wealth you have created so far. You may surprise yourself, hopefully pleasantly.

Sometimes the best way to get an idea of whether you are on track is to see a financial adviser. He or she should be able to tell you how you compare with your peers, and whether, on your present pattern of income and saving, you are likely to achieve your goals.

I have seen many clients whose perception of their wealth compared to their peers was way out of line. Some clients with considerable wealth consider themselves to be average or below-average, while others with very little wealth consider themselves to be well off.

Financial experiences

With experience comes learning. Whether your experiences are successes or failures, they will teach you plenty. The sooner you start making your own decisions about your money, the more experience you will have, the more you will learn, the more confident you will become, and the less risk-averse you will be.

You can protect yourself from failure as you experiment by surrounding yourself with experts, and learning as much as you can before you take action. This applies, in particular, to investing in property, shares or business ventures with potentially high risks.

Investing in property such as houses, apartments and commercial buildings can be an easy way to create wealth if you know how to go about it. Property ownership is familiar to most of us. It doesn't require any great skill, just a lot of knowledge that is freely available.

My advice to first-time investors is to spend several months reading, attending seminars, and researching the property market before even attempting to make a first purchase. Then, before you buy, seek advice from accountants, solicitors, other property investors or professional mentors to avoid costly mistakes. When you find an appealing property, don't let your heart rule your head. Prepare some worst-case financial projections to show how your investment will perform. At the end of the day, though, the best way to learn is to take the plunge and buy your first property.

Exactly the same principles apply to investing in shares or businesses. Do your research, talk to experts, prepare financial projections and then give it a try.

As you become more confident you will be able to take on opportunities with higher risk and a potentially higher return.

Motivation

All of us can do with more motivation from time to time – especially when the going gets tough. My own success in creating wealth has, in part, resulted from motivational techniques I have learned.

Here are some that I really recommend you try.

Document your goals in words or pictures.

Display them in a prominent place, such as on your refrigerator door or beside your bedroom mirror.

Confirm your goals daily. Say them aloud to yourself, or write them down a few times.

Meditate. Spend 15 minutes each morning or night clearing your mind and refocussing. Meditation techniques can be learnt from books and CDs, or you can attend a meditation course. If you don't feel comfortable meditating, just taking time out every day to sit and think through what you want to achieve is very useful.

Use visualisation. For example, imagine yourself as a wealthy person who has already achieved your goals. Such techniques are astonishingly powerful and are routinely used by many successful businesspeople and sportspeople around the world.

Practise positive self-talk. Tell yourself you are a successful investor with the power to create wealth.

Listen to motivational CDs. I find the perfect time to do this is on a long car journey.

8

You and your partner

ARGUMENTS ABOUT MONEY PUT HUGE STRESS ON a relationship and are a leading cause of separation and divorce. When you think about it, it's not surprising that these arguments happen. Partners in a relationship often – in fact I would say usually – have different money personalities: different levels of tolerance to risk, different priorities for spending, and different comfort zones as far as financial security goes. Unless these differences are understood and managed, arguments can be never-ending.

CASE STUDY

My clients Eric and Barbara are a good example of how different money personalities can cause problems. When they came to see me they were in their mid forties and had a debt-free home worth around $400,000.

Eric was entrepreneurial. He was determined to find innovative ways of increasing their wealth so they could build up a large retirement fund. He had attended a seminar extolling the benefits of investment in positive cash-flow property. He could see that, providing he purchased properties according to strict financial criteria, he could quickly build up a million-dollar-plus portfolio that would grow in value over time. To do this, the couple would need to borrow a million dollars by taking out a mortgage secured over the family home and the investment properties.

While Eric's financial analysis showed that, using these borrowed funds, the couple could add over $250,000 to their net wealth over the next five years, Barbara, being a hoarder, was extremely uncomfortable with the amount to be borrowed, and the fact the mortgage would be secured over the family home. The tension between Eric and Barbara grew so great that they eventually separated. While there were other factors involved in the separation, the arguments over property investment were the final straw.

CASE STUDY **ENTREPRENEUR & HOARDER**

In a relationship, differences in money personality don't have to lead to a bad outcome. In fact, once you acknowledge them they can be very useful.

Different approaches can provide a good balance between taking too much risk or too little, and between living for today or creating wealth for the future. It all comes down to how you manage the differences between you, and how well you communicate.

If the relationship between you and your partner is good in all other aspects, managing money differences should not be a problem. Understanding your partner's money personality and how it differs from your own will help you find a positive way forward. And having to discuss money matters more thoroughly and reach compromises means you can take advantage of the good points of each of your money personalities.

> Start by identifying the differences in your approaches to money, and then find solutions that keep both of you feeling comfortable.

By now you will have worked out your money personality type and that of your partner. Let's look at some possible combinations.

HOARDER & ACHIEVER

Hoarders and achievers have similar attitudes to risk, but different aspirations for wealth creation. Tension will be around how much money is spent, and what it is spent on. The achiever will want to spend on lifestyle improvements such as home renovations and new cars, even to the extent of taking on debt to do so. Increasing debt in this way will cause discomfort and worry to the hoarder, who would rather live a more frugal lifestyle without debt.

The good news

If you and your partner are a hoarder–achiever combination, through compromise you can achieve a good balance between saving and spending. Hoarders are inclined to think of money as an end in itself, rather than a means to an end. They can get so carried away with hoarding for the future that they miss out on enjoyment in the present. Luckily, the achiever will encourage them to have more fun, and the hoarder can keep the achiever's spending in check so debts don't climb too high.

HOARDER & ENTREPRENEUR

Of all the combinations, this is the most difficult. Remember Eric and Barbara? The hoarder will be aghast at the perceived recklessness of the entrepreneur, and may refuse to participate in their moneymaking schemes. The entrepreneur will feel the hoarder is holding them back, and preventing them achieving their dreams. The bitterness that results from an entrepreneur having to miss out on what later proves to have been a good opportunity can last for years, and cause a major rift in the relationship.

The good news

If you are in a hoarder–entrepreneur relationship, you and your partner should consciously decide which is more important to you – preserving wealth or preserving your relationship. The entrepreneur can reduce the hoarder's anxiety by providing thorough explanations and detailed information about wealth-creation opportunities. It may be possible, also, for the hoarder to be protected in some way from the risks of a failed venture – perhaps through the use of trusts and company structures, through not having to give personal guarantees for borrowing, and not using the family home as security. If all else fails, the fall-back position is for the couple to manage their money separately to avoid tension and conflict.

THRILL-SEEKER & HOARDER

A hoarder will consider a thrill-seeker to be an incurable spendthrift who can never keep hold of money. Conversely, a thrill-seeker will see a hoarder as someone who never has any fun, and does their best to stop him or her having fun as well. For a hoarder, the insecurity of having no funds on hand is unbearable and this will cause considerable worry and stress, whereas the thrill-seeker will be having a wonderful time spending the money the hoarder has earned and carefully saved.

The good news

The secret to making this relationship work is for the hoarder to be the chief financial controller, and for both partners to agree an amount that can be spent each week by the thrill-seeker without reference to the hoarder, on the understanding it is not to be exceeded. This can be achieved by setting low limits on credit cards, and agreeing on an amount that is paid into the thrill-seeker's personal expense account each week. The hoarder could also have funds set aside that are not immediately accessible to the thrill-seeker – for example, in a locked-in superannuation fund.

In this relationship, the thrill-seeker can have a positive impact on the hoarder by encouraging him or her to focus less on money as an end in itself, and more as a means of enjoying life.

THRILL-SEEKER & ACHIEVER

Both thrill-seekers and achievers are good at spending money rather than saving it, but an achiever will be critical of the frivolity and impulsiveness of the thrill-seeker's spending, preferring to buy things of lasting value. And thrill-seekers will find the achiever's considered, analytical approach to money frustrating. This combination can be dangerous around peak spending times such as Christmas, birthdays, holidays and major projects such as house renovation: both of you will be in the mood for spending and neither will have their eye on the bank accounts and credit cards.

The good news

Potentially a thrill-seeker and an achiever can make great things happen by combining the achiever's analytical approach with the thrill-seeker's willingness to take risk. You can identify and research opportunities for wealth creation with a balanced approach to risk-taking. Because neither of you will be particularly good at saving, you will require some external input – for example, from a professional adviser – to set up a budgeting and saving plan.

ENTREPRENEUR & ACHIEVER

Both entrepreneurs and achievers have a strong desire to create wealth, although for an entrepreneur wealth creation is a by-product of the things that really motivate them, such as success, freedom and a passion for what they do. Both like to spend money in large amounts, and there is likely to be conflict over what it is spent on. The achiever will favour lifestyle assets, while the entrepreneur will want to invest for the future. Entrepreneurs enjoy life, but given a choice between a $10,000 holiday and a $10,000 investment opportunity with a 50 percent chance of doubling their money, will choose the investment.

The good news

The achiever's conservatism will provide a good balance for the risk-taking nature of the entrepreneur, and their analytical approach will encourage the entrepreneur to do thorough homework before embarking on a new venture. With a bit of good fortune, the entrepreneur will be able to provide the lifestyle the achiever is seeking. However, entrepreneurs' fortunes are inclined to fluctuate and the achiever will need to be prepared to cut back on spending when times are tough. That is often easier said than done, particularly for an achiever who likes to maintain the impression of having significant wealth.

ENTREPRENEUR & THRILL-SEEKER

Both entrepreneurs and thrill-seekers love the satisfaction of taking a gamble and winning. The key difference is that entrepreneurs are focused on the longer term, whereas thrill-seekers want gratification now. This combination lacks the stability and commonsense of the hoarder–achiever combination. There is a real risk that wealth created by the entrepreneur will be lost by the thrill-seeker.

The good news

Life may be a bit of a roller-coaster, but you will both enjoy the ride, even if you are broke! Conflict in this relationship will arise around who makes use of any spare funds first, but this can be sorted if you agree to have some of your wealth locked away where it is not immediately accessible to either of you. This way you will have something to fall back on when times are tough, and a store of wealth for your retirement.

Working together

No matter how different your money personalities, the key to resolving conflicts is to work together on a wealth-creation plan. Set goals and objectives with which you both feel comfortable. If necessary, make some compromises and set some limits.

For the thrill-seeker, agree on a regular amount of money (either a lump sum or a percentage of income) that they are free to spend as they wish.

For the hoarder, agree on a regular amount of money (either a lump sum or a percentage of income) to be set aside in a secure place to build up a fund to cover emergencies and long-term needs.

For the achiever, agree on priorities for spending and caps on lifestyle items. For example, agree on an annual travel budget.

For the entrepreneur, agree on an amount of start-up capital for investment or a business venture, with which they can have free rein.

The power of difference

If you and your partner have different money personalities, celebrate! Think how much worse it would be if you were both the same.

Two thrill-seekers would have a lot of fun, spend a lot of money and probably have nothing left to retire on.

Two hoarders would have an uneventful life and leave behind a large inheritance for their children to spend.

Two entrepreneurs would make and lose several fortunes in their lifetime.

Two achievers would probably have the biggest house in the street and the biggest mortgage to go with it.

Different approaches to money are positive – provided you can reach good compromises.

The six easy steps to create wealth

BY NOW YOU WILL HAVE A GOOD UNDERSTANDING OF YOUR money personality and the influences that have shaped it.

You will also understand your partner's money personality, the possible areas of conflict between you, and how you can deal with them.

You will have thought about how you want to change your behaviour towards money so you can open the door to new opportunities.

It's time to start the wealth-creation process.

STEP 1

Take stock of your potential

YOUR POTENTIAL TO CREATE WEALTH IS BASED ON three things:

Your money personality

Your current net financial assets

Your current and future earning potential.

You may think you are already earning, saving or investing to your maximum. But are you really?

Money personality

Your money personality will be the dominant force in deciding how much wealth you can and want to create. By now, you will have a good understanding of the factors that have contributed to it, and how it has affected your ability to create wealth in the past.

You will have given some thought to the things about your attitude to money that you would like to change. If you have a partner, you will have explored the ways in which your money personalities differ, and how you can work together to achieve common goals.

> Now you are ready to push your boundaries and start seriously creating wealth.

Net financial assets

It goes without saying that the financial position from which you're starting will be important. If you are a 30-year-old who wants to be a millionaire by the time you are 40 and are starting with $20,000, you will need different strategies than if your current wealth is already $100,000.

In financial terms, wealth is measured by *net worth* – that is, the difference between your assets (what you own) and your liabilities (what you owe). The amount of wealth you have now will reflect how well you have managed your money in the past.

Separate your assets into two categories – lifestyle assets and investment assets. Lifestyle assets are possessions that add to your enjoyment of life but generally don't add to your wealth over time. They include such things as your house, car, boat and holiday home. These are not genuine investments as they cost money to run and maintain, do not produce a return, and – with the exception of your house and holiday home – their resale value usually drops over time.

Spending too much on lifestyle assets will lower your net worth.

Investment assets are assets that produce a return by way of income or capital gain or both. Included in this category are bonds, shares and investment property.

Contrary to what many people think, your home is *not* an investment asset. Certainly it will increase in value over time, but having too much money tied up in your home is usually not a wise strategy. Owning two properties worth $350,000 each, living in one and receiving a rental income from the other, will add more to your net wealth over time than owning one property worth $700,000, which you live in.

How much you are worth?

It is a good idea to measure your net worth from time to time. By measuring your net worth you can monitor your progress and see if you really are moving ahead. I advise my clients to do this exercise at least once a year.

It is entirely possible that your net worth could be dropping from one year to the next. This will happen if you spend more than you earn, and borrow or cash in some of your investments to make up the shortfall.

Here's a straightforward way to measure your net worth and see if you are moving ahead.

1 Make a list of all your assets and the price you could sell them for today. Include:

   lifestyle assets – such as your house, car, boat, caravan, art and antiques; and

   investment assets – such as cash deposits, shares, rental properties, business interests, superannuation funds, and the surrender value of insurance policies.

2 Next, make a list of all your borrowings – such as mortgages, personal loans and credit-card debt. List these in order according to the interest rate you are paying on each, starting with the highest rate.

3 Now add up the value of all your assets and subtract the total value of all your debt. This is your net worth, and represents the amount of value you have created during your working life.

4 Compare the value of your investment assets and your lifestyle assets. Ideally, you should keep your lifestyle assets to a minimum and have as many investment assets as possible.

5 Analyse whether your investment assets are still producing the best possible return. You will need to consider not only what their past performance has been but how you expect them to perform in the future.

   – To calculate the return over the last year, subtract the market value of the investment now from the value it had at the start of the year. This is the change in value.

   – Add to this figure the net income (after expenses and tax) that you have received from the investment during the year. This will give you the total return over the year. (If you have added more money into the investment over the year you will need to make adjustments to reflect this.)

   – Now divide the total return by the value of the investment at the start of the year. This is the percentage return from the investment over the year.

   – Compare this return with the return you expect in the future from other available investment opportunities, to assess whether you should sell or keep your investment. You should also consider whether the return compensates you for the risks you are taking.

6 Examine your debt. Have you gone into debt in this period in order to purchase investment assets – an acceptable step if the return from these assets will be greater than the cost of borrowing? Or have you borrowed just to buy lifestyle assets, and treats such as holidays?

Ideally, you should borrow as little as possible to buy lifestyle assets or things of no lasting value. These are best funded out of money you have saved.

The five golden rules for increasing net worth

1. Keep the value of your lifestyle assets to a minimum, and maximise the value of your investment assets.
2. Be cautious when spending on things such as daily living expenses, travel and cars, that have no lasting value or do not produce a return.
3. Keep your debt – and therefore your interest costs – to a minimum.
4. Look for the best possible return on the money you invest.
5. Save some of your income in order to purchase investment assets and/or reduce debt.

1 Keep the value of lifestyle assets to a minimum

A wise investor will always look for the best use of his or her money – that is, where it will achieve the best return.

Spending money on home renovations does not always add the equivalent dollar amount to a house's market value. And even if it does, you will probably get less return from $50,000 you spend on your own home than you would get by using that money for an investment – for example, as a deposit on an investment property.

> Your home is not a retirement fund.

Many people make the mistake of thinking that the more they spend on their home during their lifetime, the better off they will be when they retire. However, the idea that when you sell your home you release funds for retirement is well proven to be a myth.

I have seen this time and time again with my clients at retirement age. Most people find it difficult to reduce to a lower living standard, and while they may sell the family home for something smaller in size, the value of the home they buy is usually the same or even higher, as they want something newer and requiring less maintenance. If they purchase a house or apartment in a retirement village, they also have to set aside capital to pay ongoing charges to the village, and these can be high.

Ideally, to increase your wealth you should aim to:

- Live in a reasonably priced home.
- Use your borrowing capacity to purchase assets, such as a rental property or a business, which will produce capital gain and income.
- Over time, use the return from your investments to upgrade your home if you wish, and then borrow against the increased value of

your home to purchase even more investment assets. Alternatively, you can simply reinvest your investment income so that your investments are not encumbered with debt.

While I recommend keeping the value of your home reasonably low, I am certainly not suggesting you stay out of the property market completely. There will be a time, even if it's late in your life, when you will need your own home. The risk you run by *not* owning a home is that house prices will move out of your reach by the time you want to buy.

If you want the freedom, flexibility and lower cost of renting, consider buying an investment property that you rent to someone else, so that you have some exposure to the property market. Buying an investment property will open up more options in terms of where you can afford to buy, as you won't be restricted to the areas where you work or choose to live. If you don't like the thought of being a landlord, it's a good idea to have a property manager look after it for you.

2 Be cautious when spending

To use your money wisely, you need to be absolutely clear about the difference between 'spending' and 'investing'.

Spending is using money to purchase items that have no lasting or resale value, and that do not produce a return – for example, food, gifts, overseas travel and general living expenses.

Investing is using money to purchase items or investments that have a resale value and produce a return by way of income and/or change in value over time – for example, investment property, shares, debentures, antiques and other proven 'collectables'.

To increase your net worth, invest most and spend least.

3 Keep debt to a minimum

Paying interest is negative wealth creation. One of the best ways to get ahead financially is to keep debt to a minimum.

However, borrowing is not always bad: it depends what you are borrowing for. Net worth is the difference between total assets and total debt, so if you borrow to purchase investment assets your total debt will increase, but so will your total assets.

For example, borrowing $10,000 to buy shares that increase in value to $15,000 over time will increase your net worth. Of course, there is an element of risk in this approach as it is not possible to predict the future value of shares with accuracy.

On the other hand, borrowing to purchase items that have either no lasting value or a decreasing value will reduce your net worth. For example, borrowing to take an overseas trip will reduce your net worth by the amount you borrow.

4 Look for the best possible return

There are always options available to you as to how to invest your money. As I advised earlier, have a regular look at your net-worth calculation. Are your investment assets giving you the best possible return in relation to their risk? If the answer is no, you are not making the most of your wealth-creating opportunities.

> Every investment you make has an opportunity cost – that is, the return you would have made if you had invested the funds somewhere else.

Investments should be reviewed every year, and retained only if their present and expected future return is equal to, or better than, alternative investments with a similar level of risk – unless there are non-financial reasons for retaining them.

One of my clients inherited a large share portfolio from her father, who had been a skilled investor. Even though some of the investments needed to be sold because they were under-performing, she was reluctant to do this for sentimental reasons: she wanted to keep her father's portfolio intact.

Similarly, another client of mine who was a consultant bought shares in companies for which he undertook large projects, and kept them partly for sentimental reasons – and partly because he expected to be able to reap the rewards of his good consulting advice.

5 Save some of your income

Your ability to save has little to do with the amount of money you earn, and a lot to do with how much you spend. I have met many people with six-figure incomes who save nothing, and many with modest incomes who are good savers. Many of the people with modest incomes end up with more wealth in the long term than the people on the higher incomes.

Wealth creation starts with this basic principle:

> If you want to create wealth you must spend less than you earn.

Although this is obvious, most people don't live by it. Most of us earn one to two million dollars in our lifetime. Most of us do not know where that one to two million dollars goes.

Where is your money going?

Being aware of your total income and where it all goes is a vital step towards making the most of your money. Once you have established this, you can work on strategies to increase your level of saving – by either increasing your income or reducing your expenditure.

To get a clear picture, look at your actual income and expenditure on a month-by-month basis over the last two years. At the very least, take a three-month or six-month period and annualise it.

Income

Income includes your earnings from salary and wages, personal drawings from a business, investment income, and income from any other source.

Expenditure

Break down your expenditure into three categories.

Fixed expenditure

These are items of expenditure for which the amounts and timing of payments are known in advance, and over which you have no control unless you fundamentally change your assets or your lifestyle (for example, by selling your house). They include rates, mortgage payments, rent, insurance and vehicle registration.

Semi-fixed expenditure

These are items of expenditure that are essential but may vary in amount. For example, your phone bill will have a set amount for the rental but the toll calls will vary. Similarly, it is necessary to buy food, but there is an element of choice about whether your supermarket trolley will be filled with the basics, or include items from the deli. Other such items include power bills, car maintenance, clothing, and medical and dental costs.

Discretionary expenditure

Discretionary items are those that (in theory at least) are not essential but add to the quality of your life. They include eating at restaurants, going to the movies and taking overseas holidays.

The money-go-round

HOARDER

You will be a good saver, with a low level of debt. Any investments you have are likely to be conservative in nature, and you will feel uncomfortable with the idea of borrowing in order to invest.

THRILL-SEEKER

Chances are you are spending too much on frivolous or luxury items that have no lasting value or produce no return. You will be a poor saver, and your net-worth calculation will show little or no investment and a high level of debt. Your net worth may even be decreasing each year if you are living beyond your means. While you may be concerned about your high debt level, this won't stop you spending more.

ACHIEVER

You are probably thinking that as long as you spend on home renovations, furniture and other tangible possessions you are using your money wisely. Your net-worth calculation will show a high level of lifestyle assets and lifestyle expenditure, with a correspondingly high level of debt and low level of investment assets. Your outgoings will be high, and so you will be finding saving difficult. You may feel you are living from pay-day to pay-day.

ENTREPRENEUR

You will be focusing on building investment assets, with lifestyle assets to be acquired once you have achieved wealth and a high level of income. You may be prepared to sell your home or take out a mortgage in order to purchase or create an investment asset, such as a business or an investment property. Because you're a risk-taker, both your net worth and your income are likely to fluctuate over time, as some ventures succeed and others fail.

STEP 2

Work out what money can do for you

NO ONE EVER SAID MAKING MONEY WAS EASY. You need real motivation, so the first step is to figure out what you need money for – the great things you can achieve and enjoy if you stick to the programme. In this sense, creating wealth is not too different from training to win a marathon, or practising to excel at a musical instrument.

How many times have you committed yourself to an exercise programme – joined a gym, bought exercise equipment, purchased jogging shoes – only to find that there is always an excuse for not exercising? You don't have time, the weather is too cold, your back is playing up, there are children to be looked after – right?

Similarly, is that flute or guitar you long to learn to play lying about neglected, despite all your good intentions?

These setbacks happen because of lack of motivation. People who succeed at sport focus on how they will feel once they are fit and able to put in a strong performance. Similarly, musicians strive to meet goals they set themselves of passing examinations, performing in front of an audience, or being selected for a band or orchestra.

These benefits drive them to endure the negative aspects of their exercise or practice regime. It is no different when it comes to creating wealth.

What is the role of money in my life?

The answer to this question will depend on your values. Money may provide various things:

security

happiness

peace of mind

fun and adventure

support for family and friends

making a difference to other people's lives.

Being very clear about the role of money in your life, and what it can help you do, will give you the desire to create wealth. You will be motivated to set financial goals and work towards achieving them.

How much money do I really need?

At one extreme you may have something like a Buddhist monk approach, in which worldly possessions are merely a distraction from your quest for enlightenment, and all you require in life is food, shelter, and time for prayer and meditation.

At the other extreme, you may have an overwhelming desire to create a great deal of wealth so you can help eliminate poverty by setting up a large charitable trust.

Most people's aspirations lie somewhere between these extremes. We want a comfortable house to live in, a good education for our children, and the ability to spend money on luxuries occasionally without having to worry about where it is going to come from. We would like to be able to travel occasionally, work less as we grow older, and enjoy a comfortable and secure retirement.

Your needs will also be strongly affected by your money personality:

ACHIEVER

You are inclined to treat money as a means to acquire status symbols that reflect financial success. Your challenge is to see beyond money and status symbols, and identify the values and beliefs that are really and lastingly important to you.

ENTREPRENEUR

You are driven by success and a passion for what you do, and see money or wealth as enabling you to indulge your passion. You are the most likely of all the personality types to create wealth.

HOARDER

Security is very important to you. You tend to assume you are never going to have or make a lot of money, and you live by the motto 'Cut your coat to suit your cloth'. Your challenge is to expand your horizons and set more challenging goals, which align with your values.

THRILL-SEEKER

Money means instant gratification and you are always on the lookout for fun and excitement. As a thrill-seeker you will find it difficult to make sacrifices for long-term gain. More than any other personality type, you need to be extremely clear about the benefits you seek from money and what its role is in your life, so you have the incentive to take the steps that are necessary if you're going to achieve your goals.

CASE STUDIES

One of my clients, Mary, has a substantial investment portfolio. She uses this to provide an income so she can work only part-time and spend the rest of her week on community projects. Her priority is not to acquire more wealth, or spend money on luxuries, but to help others. Mary is happier and more enthusiastic about life than many of my clients who are focused on acquiring more material possessions or, like George whom I talked about earlier (page 3), aim to increase their wealth with no particular purpose in mind.

Another of my clients, Susie, likes to have adventure in her life. Every year she travels to a different country for a new experience, whether it's trekking through mountain villages in Peru, sailing up the Nile, or riding elephants in Thailand. Because she sees the role of money in her life as being to provide adventure, she is easily able to set goals and has no difficulty saving for her holidays. Not all her savings go towards her travel, however. As security is also important to her, she saves an equal amount of money for her retirement. Susie has a very basic lifestyle: she lives in a small house with few possessions, but has lots of friends and many interesting tales to tell.

For Mike and Jenny, educating their children is a top priority. They want to give their children the best possible start in life, and don't want them burdened with student loans. As their children are still young and it will be at least ten years before they require financial assistance for tertiary education, Mike and Jenny are saving to cover the likely costs. In effect they are allocating funds for their children that they would otherwise have put into their retirement savings; their view is that, with less debt, their children will find it easier to create wealth for themselves, and therefore not be reliant on an inheritance for their own retirement. When they retire, Mike and Jenny will be able to make full use of their accumulated capital, knowing they have already supported their children.

Francesca is an immigrant married to a New Zealander. She and her husband Ian both have good incomes, and Francesca's dream is that when she reaches the age of 55 she will be able to reduce to part-time hours so she can also work as a volunteer with new immigrants, helping them learn English and find jobs. To achieve this, she needs to find a way of supplementing her income that doesn't require time and effort on her part – for example, by building an income-producing investment portfolio.

Karl and Vanessa are a very family-oriented couple. Karl, who is ten years older than Vanessa, is an only child and his parents are in their seventies, living in rented accommodation. One of Karl's goals is to build a house with a separate flat so he can look after his parents when they are no longer able to look after themselves.

CASE STUDIES **ROLE OF MONEY**

What is the role of money in *your* life?

Perhaps you want to spend more time with your family, or help in the community? You may want to fill your life with interesting experiences through travel or education. You may have a burning cause, such as conserving and enhancing the natural environment, or helping under-privileged people.

Use this checklist to identify what money offers you.

- ◯ Financial security
- ◯ Financial freedom
- ◯ Financial independence
- ◯ A comfortable life for my family
- ◯ Support for causes, such as environmental or social
- ◯ Professional development
- ◯ Fun and excitement
- ◯ Exploration of interesting new places
- ◯ Development and practice of spirituality
- ◯ Making a difference to the lives of others
- ◯ Happiness
- ◯ A peaceful, harmonious life
- ◯ A pleasant living environment
- ◯ Personal status
- ◯ Other ______________________________

Now choose the top five. These can be called your **guiding principles**, or **personal values**.

STEP 3

Decide how much wealth you want to create

IN THE LONG RUN, WHAT HAPPENS IN LIFE IS THE RESULT of the choices we make and the goals we set and achieve. The more successful you are at setting and achieving goals, the more successful you will be – no matter how you define success.

How much wealth do you personally want to create? To find out, you need to set some goals. These will have a big influence on every major decision you make – where you live, how much you spend, what you do with your time and energy, how hard you work, and how much money you will need to save so you can ease back on work later in life.

Your goals should be consistent with your personal values. If you set goals that are not consistent, you will find that over time your values will win and you will not achieve your goals.

To understand the impact of values on goals, imagine you are a bird in the sky. If your values and goals are aligned, you will have a tail wind helping you fly to your destination. If they are contradictory, you will feel as if you are flying into a head wind and making no progress at all. If your values are only slightly consistent with your goals, you will be flying with a cross wind: you will make progress but end up in a different place from where you intended.

Write down your goals.

People who write down their goals and share them with others are far more likely to achieve them than those who don't. This is because being clear what you want gives you the focus and commitment to stay motivated.

You need to make your goals specific so you know what you have to do to achieve them. For each goal, include a dollar amount and a time-scale. For example, one of your goals may be to repay your mortgage as quickly as possible. Calculate how much you need to repay regularly, and in what time frame. If you calculate that you need to repay, say, $10,000 a year for the next ten years you will be much more likely to achieve your goal.

The compulsory goal – emergency funds

Everyone should have an emergency fund or cash buffer for unexpected or short-term expenses. If you don't already have one, this has to be your first goal.

A rule of thumb is that you should have immediate access to three months' income. For instance, if your income is $48,000 a year after tax, you should plan to have access to $12,000 at short notice.

If you still have a mortgage on your house, it doesn't pay to have this emergency money sitting in a short-term or call account that is earning less interest than you are paying on your mortgage. One way around this is to have a line of credit on your house that will be used only in an emergency. If you are a thrill-seeker, achiever or entrepreneur, you will need to discipline yourself not to use this line of credit *for any other purpose.* If you fail, you must ensure that funds used are repaid within a short period of time.

If you would prefer to have this emergency fund as a cash balance, rather than a line of credit, set a target amount for the fund and the level of saving required to achieve it, and make sure you get the highest possible rate of return when you invest it. Some banks now offer a money-management system that allows you to offset cash balances against your mortgage. This gives you the best of both worlds – you can keep your emergency funds separate from your mortgage and still minimise the interest costs on your mortgage.

Working-life goals and retirement goals

Once you have dealt with your emergency funds, there are two types of goals to consider – working-life goals and retirement goals. These reflect the two major stages of life. Retirement is defined here as the time at which you will cease earning the majority of your income through working. This can be at any age, young or old.

There are several reasons to separate these two stages. In retirement, the ability to generate additional wealth through effort is substantially reduced. We are usually mainly or wholly reliant on passive income, and if we lose part of our wealth for any reason it is difficult to replace it.

You cannot, therefore, rely on creating the wealth in retirement that you need to achieve your retirement goals. During your working life, you need to create sufficient wealth to achieve your working-life goals *and* your retirement goals.

Working-life goals

Your working-life goals should cover all the important areas of your life:

personal development

health, fitness and wellbeing

spirituality

relationships with partner, family and friends

career and business

social life

community involvement

anything else that is important to you.

Each of your goals should include a dollar value and a time scale. For example, an annual adventurous holiday may cost around $5,000. For your children's university education, you may require a lump sum of $20,000 in ten years' time to repay a student loan.

Here are some examples:

Guiding principle	Working-life goal
Achieve financial freedom	Buy a business within five years that will generate personal income of $100,000 per year
Be financially secure	Pay off mortgage of $100,000 within three years
Live in a comfortable environment	Build a house with a value of $500,000 within five years

To achieve each of your working-life goals you will need to save a certain amount annually. If your savings earned no interest, the amount you would need to save would be the total divided by the number of years. For example, to save $10,000 in 20 years you would need to save $500 a year.

Fortunately, however, the compounding of interest works in your favour, and greatly reduces the amount you need to save.

Assuming a modest rate of return of 3% after taxes and fees on the money you save, the following table shows the amount you will need to save each year to accumulate $10,000 over various time frames:

Savings period	Annual saving to accumulate $10,000
5 years	$1883
10 years	$872
15 years	$534
20 years	$372
25 years	$274
30 years	$210
35 years	$165
40 years	$133

This shows clearly the benefits of compound interest. For example, on a 20-year time frame, instead of having to save $500 a year to reach a total of $10,000, you need to save only $372.

If you need to save a bigger or smaller amount than $10,000, multiply the saving amount accordingly. For example, you need to save $20,000 in ten years. Simply multiply $872 x 2: you will need to save $1744 a year. If you need to save $5000 in 15 years, you will need to save $534 x 0.5, or $267 a year.

Your working-life goals should be divided into medium-term goals (within five years) and long-term goals (longer than five years), because you will need different investment strategies for each.

Retirement goals

In addition to working-life goals, we all need retirement goals. Even if you don't plan to stop working altogether, it is likely that you will one day want to work less and have more leisure time. You will want to ensure you have enough money to fulfil the goals you have for this later stage of your life.

Some of these goals can be paid for from income, and some will require capital. For planning purposes, it is useful to distinguish between the two. Usually items paid from income are smaller and more frequent, whereas items funded from capital are larger, and one-off or infrequent.

Here's how your retirement goals may look.

The purpose of money in my retirement	Retirement goal	Cost	Income or capital?
Financial security	Retain money in a savings account for emergency purposes.	$10,000	Capital
A comfortable living environment	Replace car and whiteware on retirement.	$50,000	Capital
Interesting experiences	Travel overseas for three months before the age of 70.	$40,000	Capital
Fun with family and friends	Dine out with friends twice a month and go to concerts four times a year.	$4,000	Income
	Travel to visit family once a year.	$3,000	Income

There are three steps involved in planning your retirement.

1. Calculate how much annual income you will need.
2. Calculate how much capital you will need to produce this income.
3. Calculate how much money you will need to save each year between now and retirement to create this capital.

Of course, if you are many years away from lessening your workload or retiring, inflation will alter the amount you require. The best way to deal with this is to assume that all your calculations are in today's dollars, and adjust for inflation each year. Your target retirement income and capital will go up by the amount of inflation for that year, as will the amount of saving you need to do to produce the capital you require. It is easier to work in today's dollars because the numbers are more meaningful.

Calculate your retirement income

To calculate how much annual income you will need in retirement, first identify what you will need for basic living costs. A useful guide is the annual government pension currently paid to superannuitants.

Current rates for New Zealand Superannuation can be found on the website *www.winz.govt.nz*. New Zealand Superannuation is designed to provide a basic lifestyle, so the amount is a guide to what your day-to-day living expenses would be, assuming you have a debt-free home and no dependants.

There are two other ways to calculate how much income you will need to cover basic living costs. One is to take a percentage – for example, 70% – of the income you currently earn. This works well for people on an average income, but not necessarily so well for those on a very high or very low income.

A more time-consuming approach is to draw up a detailed budget for retirement living costs, based on the assumption that you will have no dependants and your mortgage will probably be paid off.

Once you have calculated these basic living costs, add the amount of income you will need to cover those of your retirement goals that will be paid for from income.

Here is what an annual retirement-income calculation looks like for Peter and Helen, a 50-year-old couple who are planning their retirement.

Retirement goal	Cost
Basic living costs	$20,000
Annual holiday in New Zealand or Australia	$3,000
Entertainment and dining out	$4,000
Home improvements and maintenance	$2,000
Sports club/gym membership fees	$1,000
Total	**$30,000**

Calculate your retirement capital

The amount of capital you will need when you are working less, or not at all, depends on the amount of income you will need – as calculated in the example above – minus your government pension and any other pension you expect to receive. If you wish to provide for your own retirement rather than rely on there being a government pension for which you will be eligible, you should make no deduction for this.

Once you have determined how much income you will need, you can calculate how much capital is required to produce it. First, though, you will need to make some assumptions about:

The age at which you wish to have the option to stop working (even though you may still choose to work).

The age to which you expect to live. This can be based on statistical averages – around 82 for a female and 77 for a male – or on your family history of longevity.

How much of an inheritance you wish to leave for your children. The larger the amount the more retirement capital you will need, because you will be less able to use your capital as a way of creating income.

For example, you may anticipate a retirement period of 20 years and a rate of return of 3% after tax on your capital, and you may want to leave an inheritance of $50,000 (excluding the value of your house).

This table shows how much retirement capital you will need to produce various levels of annual income from your investments (that is, over and above your pension income).

Annual income required from investments	Retirement capital required
$5,000	$104,000
$10,000	$108,000
$15,000	$258,000
$20,000	$334,000

To this amount, add the amount of capital required to cover your retirement goals that will be funded from capital.

CASE STUDY

Peter and Helen's reckoning looks like this.

Step One – Calculate income required from investments:

Annual income required	$30,000
Minus pension income	$20,000
Income required from investments	$10,000

Step Two – Calculate total retirement capital required:

Retirement capital required for income of $10,000	$108,000
Plus capital needed for spending at retirement:	
New car	$20,000
New whiteware	$2,000
Overseas trip	$30,000
Total retirement capital required	**$160,000**

CASE STUDY **RETIREMENT CAPITAL**

Calculate how much you need to save for retirement

Once you know how much capital you need to accumulate by the time you retire, you can calculate the annual savings required to achieve that target from any given age. You may plan to start saving for your retirement now, or you may decide to delay until you have repaid your mortgage, or your children have left home.

> The longer you leave it to start saving for retirement, the more you will have to save each year to reach your target. If you start early, you will have to save only a small amount.

To calculate how much you need to save:

1 Work out how much your present savings (if you have any) will be worth by the time you retire, or start working less. This table shows the value of $10,000 invested at a return of 3% after tax for various periods of time.

	Time period invested				
	5 years	10 years	15 years	20 years	25 years
$10,000 invested	$13,049	$16,583	$20,680	$25,431	$30,938

Peter and Helen plan to retire in 15 years. They have already saved $50,000. By investing this money at 3%, they will have $103,400 in 15 years time ($20,680 x 5).

2 Subtract the future value of your present savings from the total amount of retirement capital you need.

Peter and Helen need $160,000 by the time they retire. The $50,000 they have already saved will be worth $103,400. They will, therefore, need an additional $56,600.

3 Calculate how much you need to save to reach your target amount of capital.

This table shows how much you need to save each year to accumulate $10,000 over different periods of time, assuming a 3% after-tax return on your investments.

Savings period	Annual saving to accumulate $10,000
5 years	$1,883
10 years	$872
15 years	$534
20 years	$372
25 years	$274
30 years	$210
35 years	$165
40 years	$133

You can use this table to work out the savings you need to make for multiples of $10,000. For example, if you need to accumulate $100,000, multiply the numbers in the table by 10.

Peter and Helen need a total of $160,000 in retirement capital. After allowing for the future value of their current investments, they will need an additional $56,600. Using this table, they will need to save an additional $3,022 a year ($534 x 5.66) to reach their target.

CASE STUDY

This is Peter and Helen's retirement savings plan.

- They start with a lump sum of $50,000.
- By investing this at 3% after-tax return and adding to it at the rate of $3,022 a year for the next 15 years, they will retire at the age of 65 with a lump sum of $160,000 of which they will spend $52,000.
- When invested at a return of 3% after tax, this will generate an income of $10,000 a year for them for 20 years as an addition to New Zealand Superannuation. This income will be a combination of investment return and capital.
- After 20 years, they will have $50,000 left in capital.

CASE STUDY **RETIREMENT SAVINGS PLAN**

The mortgage factor

If you have a mortgage, you may wish to wait until it is fully paid off before you start saving for retirement.

Here's an example:

You are 35 and plan to retire in 30 years, at age 65. You decide to use all your savings for the next 15 years to eliminate your mortgage. Your retirement savings period will then be 15 years, starting at age 50.

Paying off your mortgage before saving for retirement should be considered only in certain circumstances. See page 151 for more information on whether you should save or pay off debt.

Making it simple

If you find this retirement calculation method too complicated, take a short cut by using one of the many retirement calculators available on the internet (for example, the quick calculator on *www.sorted.org.nz*), or by using the following table as a guide.

This shows how much money you will need to save each *month* to make up the difference between your estimated annual income requirement and what you will receive from government superannuation and/or any other pension to which you may be entitled. It assumes you will retire at 65 and require 20 years of retirement income.

	Age when saving starts							
Annual income additional to government and other pensions	**25**	**30**	**35**	**40**	**45**	**50**	**55**	**60**
$5,000	65	84	110	148	207	308	514	1,138
$10,000	130	167	220	296	414	616	1,027	2,277
$15,000	195	251	330	444	621	924	1,541	3,415
$20,000	260	335	440	594	828	1,232	2,054	4,554
$25,000	324	419	550	740	1,035	1,540	2,568	5,692
$30,000	389	502	660	888	1,242	1,848	3,082	6,831
$35,000	454	586	770	1,036	1,450	2,156	3,595	7,969
$40,000	519	670	880	1,185	1,657	2,464	4,109	9,108
$45,000	584	754	990	1,333	1,864	2,772	4,622	10,246
$50,000	649	837	1,099	1,481	2,071	3,080	5,136	11,385

These figures assume a return of 4% after fees and taxes on your investment *before* you retire, and 3% after fees and taxes *after* you retire. There has been no adjustment for inflation, or for other investments or savings you may have. The figures assume you will use up all your capital over the 20 years of retirement.

Source: Tower New Zealand

KiwiSaver and other subsidised retirement savings schemes

In New Zealand, KiwiSaver is an incentivised retirement savings scheme introduced by the government. If you join you receive a lump-sum contribution from the government. You are also entitled to an annual tax credit, and a compulsory employer contribution equal to 4% of your pay.

> The government and employer contributions to your KiwiSaver scheme reduce the amount of retirement savings you need to make from your own resources.

Some employers also offer their own subsidised retirement savings schemes. If you are a member of one of these schemes, you should deduct from your required saving the total annual contributions made by your employer and/or the government.

Returning to Peter and Helen, let's assume that Peter is a member of KiwiSaver, and that his total KiwiSaver contributions from him, his employer and the government are $3,000 per annum ($1,000 from each). We have calculated that Peter and Helen need to save $3,022 a year for the next 15 years to reach their required retirement capital. Deducting the $3,000 KiwiSaver contributions from this figure means they have to save only another $22 a year to reach their target.

More information on KiwiSaver is provided on pages 227–230.

Putting it all together

Now that you have set your goals and put figures on them, let's bring them all together to see the total picture. How much wealth do you need to live the life you want?

- Identify your goals, and give them a dollar value and time frame.
- Make up a spreadsheet, listing your medium-term goals and long-term goals down the left-hand side, and years across the top.
  - Your medium-term goals will consist of your compulsory emergency fund and your medium-term working-life goals (to be achieved within five years).
  - Your long-term goals will consist of your long-term working-life goals (to be achieved in five years or more) and your retirement goals.
- Now record the savings you will need to make each year between now and retirement to achieve each of your goals.

> Quantifying the amounts on a time-line gives you a clear set of goals to achieve, and helps you get a feel for what is realistically achievable.

The table on the next page is called a **savings planner**. In this example we can see how my clients Warren and Kay set and quantified their goals.

	Warren and Kay's savings planner	Year 1	Year 2	Year 3	Year 4	Year 5	Year 6	Year 7	Year 8	Year 9	Year 10	Year 11
Medium-term goals	*Emergency fund*											
	Establish a fund of $10,000 within 5 years	$1,883	$1,883	$1,883	$1,883	$1,883						
	Working-life goals – medium-term											
	Take the family on an overseas holiday in 5 years' time at a cost of $20,000	$3,766	$3,766	$3,766	$3,766	$3,766						
	Dine out once a month at a cost of $1,200 per year	$1,200	$1,200	$1,200	$1,200	$1,200	$1,200	$1,200	$1,200	$1,200	$1,200	$1,200
	Total medium-term saving	**$6,849**	**$6,849**	**$6,849**	**$6,849**	**$6,849**	**$1,200**	**$1,200**	**$1,200**	**$1,200**	**$1,200**	**$1,200**
Long-term goals	*Working-life goals – long-term*											
	Give daughter $10,000 towards student loan in 8 years' time	$1,125	$1,125	$1,125	$1,125	$1,125	$1,125	$1,125	$1,125			
	Give son $10,000 towards student loan in 10 years' time	$872	$872	$872	$872	$872	$872	$872	$872	$872	$872	
	Retirement goals											
	Save $200,000 for retirement in 15 years' time, commencing in 5 years' when the mortgage is repaid						$17,440	$17,440	$17,440	$17,440	$17,440	$17,440
	Total long-term saving	**$1,997**	**$1,997**	**$1,997**	**$1,997**	**$1,997**	**$19,437**	**$19,437**	**$19,437**	**$18,312**	**$18,312**	**$17,440**
	Total saving required	**$8,846**	**$8,846**	**$8,846**	**$8,846**	**$8,846**	**$20,637**	**$20,637**	**$20,637**	**$19,512**	**$19,512**	**$18,640**

Being realistic

Are your goals realistic? As well as fitting your life vision, they need to be consistent with your money personality.

The savings you will need to achieve them will have to come from either your income or from the wealth you create through your investments. And the amount of wealth you will be able to create will ultimately depend on whether you are a hoarder, an achiever, an entrepreneur or a thrill-seeker.

If you have found you will need to triple your current wealth in ten years, this may not be a problem if you are an entrepreneur, but is likely to be unrealistic if you are a hoarder or a thrill-seeker. If you are an achiever, you will achieve it only by curbing your levels of spending.

If your goals are unrealistic, you need to either change them or stretch the limits of your money personality – for example by changing your attitude towards risk, and towards money and wealth-creation in general.

> It is good to set targets that take you outside your comfort zone. You may be able to achieve a lot more than you thought possible.

STEP 4

Find ways to create wealth

IF YOU HAVE FOLLOWED THE STEPS IN THE PREVIOUS chapter you now know how much money you need to have to achieve your goals for your working life, for easing back on work or retiring, and for emergencies.

Of course, your priorities will change through your lifetime. You may develop new interests, and your family circumstances or your health may change. You may even have a mid-life crisis and turn your life upside down. When this happens you will need to review your goals and the money you will need to achieve them. You should always have a clear view of where you are heading.

Different ways of creating wealth suit different money personalities. Be sure to take this into account.

There are five ways to create wealth:

Cut costs and save without sacrificing your lifestyle

Create more net income with little effort

Use technology to create wealth automatically

Multiply your money

Protect your nest egg.

Cut costs and save without sacrificing your lifestyle

To save, you have to spend less than you earn.

Hoarders, who live by the motto 'Cut your coat to suit your cloth', have no difficulty keeping their costs within their income. My client Andrea is a good example. A single woman of 64, she has no children at home and no mortgage so her expenses are low. Her unemployment benefit gives her around $9,000 a year after tax. In a few months' time, when she turns 65, she will be eligible for New Zealand Superannuation, and her income will increase to around $13,000 a year after tax. She tells me that she will then be able to save $4,000 per annum.

This is in stark contrast to **thrill-seeker** David, who is also single, has no children at home and is renting a flat. For thrill-seekers, life is just one big spending spree. David has an after-tax income of $60,000, but he spends all his income travelling, eating out, drinking expensive wines and gambling at casinos. He has not saved and now, at age 52, is worrying about how he is going to support his lifestyle on $13,000-a-year superannuation when he retires.

> If you are a thrill-seeker and need to save, you must put strict limits on your spending.

Entrepreneurs, like hoarders, often have a frugal lifestyle. True entrepreneurs live in the future: they imagine themselves already living their vision. They see their present lifestyle as a temporary stepping-stone to their ultimate lifestyle, which they know with certainty they will achieve.

For status-conscious **achievers**, the challenge is to live the life of luxury to which you aspire, without spending a fortune. Take Christine and John. A professional couple with two children, between them they earn around $100,000 after tax, yet they have not been able to save. They live in a prestigious suburb and send their children to private schools. A large part of their income goes on paying school fees and a large mortgage.

Focusing on ways to cut costs, Christine and John decided that sending their children to private schools was important to them, but they could save money by selling their house and moving to a lower priced suburb, thus reducing their mortgage.

> If you are an achiever, focus on making your dollars stretch further.

Buy good quality items when they are discounted, and spend money on things that have real value, rather than just being status symbols.

The Savings Equation

Based on the fact that income can be only spent or saved, the Savings Equation says:

Income =
daily living expenses + medium-term savings + long-term savings.

In this equation:

Income is your after-tax income from all sources, including employment, benefits and investment income.

Daily living expenses are the items on which you spend money each pay-day.

Medium-term savings are the money you set aside regularly to cover your emergency funds and medium-term working-life goals – that is, the goals you wish to achieve within the next ten years.

Long-term savings cover both your long-term working-life goals and your retirement goals. If you have followed the steps on pages 97–108, you will know how much money you need to be saving to achieve your goals.

By definition, your Savings Equation has to balance, unless you borrow to make up the difference. If all your money is being used for daily living expenses, you are not saving and will not be able to achieve your goals.

Write down your Savings Equation:

Net income 1	$	Daily living expenses	$
Net income 2	$	Medium-term savings	$
Net income 3	$	Long-term savings	$
Total net income	**$**	**Total outgoings**	**$**

Does your equation balance? If it doesn't, you need to make at least one of these changes:

- Reduce or eliminate some of your goals.
- Reduce your daily living expenses.
- Increase your net income.

How to save more

It is entirely possible to become wealthy on an average wage. All you have to do is follow a few simple rules.

Rule 1 – *Don't worry about your income: worry about how high your spending is relative to your income.*

Someone who earns $100,000 a year and spends $105,000 is in a worse position long-term than someone who earns $35,000 a year and spends $30,000.

Rule 2 – *Wipe all unimportant items from your budget.*

You have a choice about what you spend money on. Spend it only on things that are important to you and cut out all the rest. This is easier than you may think. For example, making your own lunch to take to work, rather than buying lunch, could save you $30 to $40 a week.

Rule 3 – *When spending money, spend as little as possible on things that have no lasting value, and as much as possible on things that will increase in value.*

Someone who spends $10,000 on a car and invests $25,000 will be much better off after five years than someone who spends $35,000 on a car and invests nothing.

Rule 4 – *Start saving sooner rather than later. Time is not standing still, and neither should you.*

Saving is like going on a journey. If you want to travel 600 kilometres and have ten hours in which to do it, you can take a safe, leisurely trip at 60 kilometres per hour. If you have only three hours, you will need to travel at a reckless 200 kilometres per hour.

The same applies to saving. To retire with $150,000, you can save at a slower rate, and with less risk, if you have 45 years to retirement rather than only ten.

Leaky bucket syndrome

People who are poor savers usually suffer from what I call 'leaky bucket syndrome'. Imagine you have a bucket into which all your money goes when you earn it. Imagine that bucket has a number of small holes. Through these small holes, money disappears in small amounts – a few dollars here, a few dollars there. After a period of time, there is no money left in the bucket, and little evidence of where it has gone.

The majority of poor savers don't spend money in large amounts. They spend it in small amounts on a large number of items – a latte, a movie, a video hire for the kids, an ice-cream, a couple of plants for the garden, a bottle of wine.

Leaky bucket syndrome is largely caused by a lack of clear goals. This, in turn, is caused by a lack of understanding of the role of money in your life. If you have clear goals and are motivated to achieve them, you will think twice about spending money on things that don't help you progress towards these goals.

The impact of leaky bucket syndrome is both immediate and long-term. If you spend $12 today on two glasses of wine, not only have you lost the value of that $12 immediately, you have also lost the compound interest you would have earned on that $12 for every year thereafter.

The miracle of compound interest

You may think that saving a few extra dollars a week is not going to make a lot of difference to your wealth. But let's say you cut out just a few items from your weekly spend.

Takeaway coffee	$15
Takeaway lunch	$30
Lottery ticket	$10
Bottle of wine	$15
Total weekly saving	**$70**

Let's say you invest that $70 a week at a return of 5% per annum compounded. After 10 years you will have accumulated $47,198, after 15 years $81,262 and after 20 years $124,995.

Revise your budget

Look at how you currently spend money, and identify some areas where you can save. Think again about what is important to you and what is not. By cutting back on discretionary items such as dining out, video hire, magazines and expensive gifts, you may be able to save enough to afford the holiday of your dreams.

Compile a list of things on which you currently spend money. We looked at this in 'Where is your money going?' on page 84. Go back to that list and circle the items on which you can cut back, or do without entirely.

Set yourself a limit as to how much you are going to spend on daily living expenses. Make sure the amount is less than your income, so you are able to save.

Now divide that into the same three categories we used before, but keep the total within the limit you have set.

Fixed expenditure

These are items where the amounts and timing of payments are known in advance, and you have no control over them unless you fundamentally change your assets or your lifestyle (for example, by selling your house). They include rates, insurance and vehicle registration.

Semi-fixed expenditure

These are items that are essential but may vary in amount. For example, your phone bill will have a set amount for the rental, but the toll calls will vary. Similarly, it is necessary to buy groceries, but you can choose whether to fill the trolley with basics, or with items from the deli.

Discretionary expenditure

Discretionary items are those that, in theory, are not essential at all, but that add to our quality of life. They include eating in restaurants, going to the movies, and attending high-priced sporting matches.

> Make your new budget as detailed as you can.

Reduce the amount of interest you pay

One of your biggest expenses will probably be the interest on your mortgage and other debts. Why pay more in interest than you have to? This table shows how much interest you pay on a $5,000 debt if you pay it off at $100 a month.

Interest rate	Time taken to pay off the debt	Interest paid (approximate)
10%	65 months	$1,500
15%	79 months	$2,900
20%	108 months	$5,800

Here's how you can reduce the interest you pay.

Step 1 – *Stop adding to your debt.*

- Hide your credit cards. Better still, put them in a containerful of water in the freezer. By the time they thaw out, you will have had second thoughts about getting into more debt.
- Delay your next big purchase if it is not utterly essential.
- Postpone your holiday, or take a cheaper one.

Step 2 – *Make a list of all your current debts.*

Start with the one that has the highest interest rate and moving down to one with the lowest. Your list will include credit-card debt, personal loans (for example, car loans), student loans and mortgages.

Step 3 – *Find ways to refinance your debts at a lower rate.*

Get on the phone and search the internet. You may be surprised to find that there are many different rates available from banks and other lending institutions. Here are some options:

- Mortgages usually have a lower interest rate than credit cards and hire purchase. You may be able to increase your mortgage to repay credit-card debt or an item you have bought on hire purchase.

- Assets other than your house – for example, car, boat, insurance policy, furniture and computer equipment – can also be used as security for a loan, so you can borrow at a lower interest rate than for an unsecured debt. Shop around credit-card providers to see if you can get a lower rate of interest.

- Contact a finance company that offers debt-consolidation to see if you can reduce your interest cost. Bear in mind that, with some of your debt, there may be penalties if you repay early: check on this before you proceed. Also be aware that additional costs – such as administration and insurance – may be added to your debt if you refinance. These can add considerably to the cost of debt.

Step 4 – *Using the savings you've identified, commit to setting aside an amount of your income each week for debt repayment.*

When repaying, start with the debt at the top of your list – the one with the highest interest rate. Keep payments on the other debts at the minimum level, and plough all your spare cash into reducing the debt at the top of your list by increasing your regular payments, making lump sum payments, or both.

Resist temptation

One of the dangers of refinancing to get rid of credit-card and finance-company debt is that, as soon as the debt has been moved, you will go out and make more purchases on credit. This can start a vicious cycle where you have to keep increasing your mortgage to get rid of expensive short-term debt.

To prevent this happening, you need to be really disciplined with your spending. Here are two good ways.

- Cut the limit on your credit card to a very low amount, if you don't want to stop using it altogether.
- Set up an automatic payment into a savings account, so you get into the habit of saving the money you need to make a purchase, rather than buying the item on credit.

Get out of a debt trap

If you have a large amount of short-term debt at high rates of interest, and no assets against which the debt can be secured, you are probably in a debt trap. The repayments on your debt are so high you need to go into more debt to keep up with them.

When your total borrowing is high, lenders will also probably demand that you buy debt-repayment insurance, and this will add to your total debt.

If you are in a debt trap you may be faced with either bankruptcy or taking on additional employment to try and meet your debt commitments. The financial pressure often leads to stress, depression and relationship breakdown.

This situation usually arises if you have been living beyond your means, although failed businesses, failed relationships that result in division of assets and loss of income, gambling and drug problems can also be factors.

> Thrill-seekers and entrepreneurs are the personalities most likely to find themselves in a debt trap.

CASE STUDY

When they came to see me, John and Sue had a load of debts.

Credit-card debt of $1,000 at 18.95%

Finance company loan of $20,000 at 14.9%

Mortgage of $28,000 at 7.4%

Mortgage of $143,000 at 6.5%

Finance company loan of $4,400, interest-free providing it was paid back within 18 months.

They were spending around $1,900 a month servicing this debt, and as Sue was not working in paid employment they were struggling to keep up with payments.

Not only were they paying a high rate of interest on some of their debt, they had to pay off principal over a short term. They were having to add to their credit-card debt (at 18.95% interest) to keep up the payments on their other loans. The stress of trying to make ends meet was getting to be too much.

Fortunately for John and Sue, their house had a value of $310,000, so we were able to increase their mortgage to repay the expensive short-term debt. The mortgage repayments were set at an amount they could afford, and they were hopeful of being able to make additional payments from time to time to get rid of the mortgage as quickly as possible.

CASE STUDY **DEBT TRAP**

To escape from a debt trap, you have to get your debt repayments to a level that is achievable, with enough cash left over to pay for living costs. I recommend the following:

- Refinance your debts at the lowest possible interest rate, and spread repayments over a longer period.
- If your debt levels are so high that you can't find a lender willing to refinance the debt, seek help from a family member or close friend, who is able to provide a guarantee or some form of security. It is essential that this person is aware of the financial risk involved.
- If you still have difficulty meeting repayments, try and reach an agreement with your lenders on a repayment schedule that is affordable for you. They will usually prefer to accommodate you, rather than have to write off the debt through bankruptcy.

In New Zealand, you can apply to the Court for a Summary Instalment Order. This will set out a manageable payment schedule so your creditors can be repaid over a period of up to three years. Payments will be made weekly from your wages or benefit, and a supervisor will be appointed to oversee the process and help you manage your debt payments. You will not be charged interest on your debts from the time the order is made. Most other countries have a similar process.

As well as restructuring your payments, you should be looking at ways of either increasing your income to service your debts, or making drastic cuts in your spending.

> If you are in a debt trap, it is always good to consult a budget advice service.

New Zealand has a network under the umbrella of the Federation of Family Budgeting Services *www.familybudgeting.org.nz*. This is a free service.

Good debt v. bad debt

Not all debt is bad. If you have borrowed money to purchase an asset that produces an income or a return higher than the interest costs, your debt will be helping you create wealth. And in many cases the interest costs will be tax-deductible.

Say you borrow $100,000 to purchase a share portfolio. You pay $10,000 a year in interest, and your share portfolio produces a gross return of $15,000 – $5,000 in dividends and a $10,000 increase in the value of the shares.

Assuming you are not considered by the tax department to be a share trader, the $10,000 capital gain on your shares will not be taxable. The dividends of $5,000 *will* be taxable, but against this you can offset the interest costs of $10,000, leaving you with a tax loss of $5,000.

If you are on a 33% tax rate, you will have a tax benefit of $1,650 – that is, 33% of $5,000.Your net return after tax will therefore be $6,650 ($15,000 less $10,000 plus $1,650).

Bearing in mind that you have invested no money of your own to generate the $6,650 (it was all borrowed), this is a windfall profit.

Of course there is always a catch, and that is the investment risk that you take on. Your investment could have produced a return that was less than the interest cost, or even negative, so risks need to be carefully calculated before you borrow to invest.

Tips for cutting costs

HOARDER

Keeping your spending to a minimum is something at which you excel. Just make sure you are not being *too* frugal.

ACHIEVER

Focus on plugging the holes in your leaky bucket.

- Set a definite limit on how much you spend on discretionary items – and stick to it.
- Learn to be frugal. Buy only what you need and find the best value for money.
- Learn to distinguish between what really are essential items and what are not. While you may think it essential to buy a coffee every morning on the way to work, you'll save a lot of money brewing a cup in the office.

ENTREPRENEUR

If you are a true entrepreneur, and not an achiever in disguise, cutting back on expenses will not be an issue. If anything, you are more likely to deprive yourself and your family of luxuries so you have enough money for your entrepreneurial activities.

THRILL-SEEKER

Your leaky bucket is more of a sieve. Your expenditure doesn't just need cutting, it needs slashing drastically. A big chunk of your income will be going on fixed expenses relating to debt repayment, and you may have little available for discretionary expenses. To free up enough cash to repay debt faster, you may have to cut back on essentials such as food, power and phone. Also:

- Put your credit cards on ice and take a holiday from spending.
- Make a commitment to put a set amount each week into debt repayment, starting with the debt with the highest interest rate.

Tips for everyone

- Cut back on your grocery bill by reducing the frequency of your visits to the supermarket and buying only goods on your shopping list.
- Take advantage of prompt-payment discounts on bills and avoid late-payment penalties. With regular accounts such as phone and power, this is easily achieved by signing up for direct-debit payments.
- Review and update your insurance policies. Are you paying more for insurance cover than you need to?
- Set a dollar limit for each gift you buy – and stick to it.
- Take lunch to work three or four days a week.
- Set up separate personal spending accounts for you and your partner – to keep a limit on the total amount you each spend.

Now you have revised your budget for daily living expenses, look at your Savings Equation. Are you saving enough to achieve your goals? If not, you need to adjust your goals, further reduce your daily living expenses – or create more net income. Read on!

Create more net income

There are many ways to create additional net income.

- Ask for and get a pay rise.
- Find a new job on a higher rate of pay.
- Undertake further training so you can move into a more highly paid position.
- Take on extra work.
- Add some passive income.
- If you are on a high rate of tax, find ways of reducing the amount of tax you pay.

These are all safe strategies with which even hoarders will feel comfortable. Then there is this:

- Borrow to invest. This can be a way of both reducing your tax and adding to your net income. It will suit entrepreneurs, for whom it is a natural course of action. Thrill-seekers will need to be cautious and get good advice before they plunge in. Hoarders and achievers may not be comfortable with borrowing to invest.

Get a pay rise

Are you being paid what you're worth? Have you had a pay rise lately?

When was the last time you looked at what people in similar jobs are being paid?

Check with recruitment consultants. They will be aware of current market rates.

Never ignore an opportunity to apply for a promotion. Even if unsuccessful, you are signalling to your employer that you are keen to move ahead.

Find a new job

Are you in a rut? Another way of raising your earnings is to change employer from time to time. Of course, this needs to be weighed up against the disadvantages of changing jobs – for example, the stress associated with learning a new job and fitting into a new workplace – but long-term you may be much better off.

Undertake further training

Is there an opportunity to increase your earnings by investing in yourself? You may be able to take a course that will give you access to a higher paying career. Think carefully, though, before you take on a large student loan in mid-life. To recoup the investment in both loan debt and lost earnings may take more years than you have left in the workforce – but of course there may be other benefits besides money that make such study well worthwhile.

Take on extra work

Can you take on extra work? A good strategy for saving for a specific purpose – for example, to repay a large credit-card debt or save for a holiday – is to take on a small additional part-time job.

Add some passive income

An increasingly popular way of getting more income is to develop passive income – that is, income you can earn with very little or no effort. Generating income that is, truly passive is not easy. Unless it comes purely from an investment, an income usually requires some effort to make it sustainable.

There are plenty of network marketing schemes that promise passive income, but the percentage of people who end up earning significant amounts from these schemes is low. To succeed, you will need very well-developed sales skills.

Here are some examples of passive income:

- Sell the intellectual property rights to a book, an invention or a business idea.
- Franchise your business.
- Purchase a business or a rental property and employ someone to manage it.

You can find more information on investing in businesses and property on pages 237–59.

Other ways to increase your income

- Sell unwanted goods and outgrown children's toys on the internet – through eBay, TradeMe or similar websites.
- In your spare time, operate a small business from home – such as direct-marketing (including telemarketing), gardening, lawn-mowing, child care, housework or office work. Use the internet to promote this business. The internet has exponentially expanded the ways goods and services can be sold, creating unlimited opportunities for new businesses – and for people with skills to provide internet-based services for them.
- Find ways of making money from a hobby you enjoy. If you are a gardener, sell surplus seedlings. If you are a train enthusiast, sell photos of trains to other enthusiasts. If you are a cook or craft-worker, make goods to sell at street fairs and farmers' markets. Find old pieces of furniture that need repairing, restore them and sell them. Again, use the internet to sell your products.
- Take in a boarder, such as a foreign student.

CASE STUDY

One of my clients, a divorced woman in her fifties, has a steady stream of young boarders staying with her. Not only does this help her pay the bills and save for retirement, she also gets lots of pleasure from the young people, whom she treats as if they are her own children. She never needs to advertise for people as most of her boarders come by word of mouth.

To accommodate more people, she has made alterations to her house. This is a clever move: the cost is being covered by the extra board she receives, and she has added value – and therefore future capital gain – to her property.

Nicky and Alan have ambitious plans to grow their wealth so they can build the house of their dreams, but with young children and a single income they are struggling to see how they can achieve them.
Nicky talks to some of her friends about how she can earn money from home. Soon she has a phone call from a friend of a friend. Would Nicky be interested in looking after her two children during the day while she is at work? Another acquaintance turns out to be looking for a place for her daughter to board for a while, because the daughter is not getting on with the woman's new partner. Through talking to others, Nicky has found a way of making $500 a week with little additional cost or effort.

CASE STUDY **CREATING MORE INCOME**

Reduce the amount of tax you pay

In an egalitarian society, tax is used as a mechanism to redistribute wealth from people on high incomes to those at the other end of the scale. Tax departments take a dim view of tax avoidance, and have wide-ranging powers to undo financial and other arrangements that have been put in place to deliberately avoid paying tax, and to impose penalties on the perpetrators. However, taxpayers are able to take reasonable steps to ensure they do not pay too much tax and are able to take advantage of tax benefits.

When it comes to savings and investments, there are a number of ways investors can ensure tax minimisation. Before you make any decisions you should seek advice from an accountant or tax expert. Tax laws vary between countries and are constantly changing. Not only that, but they require interpretation: tax laws are rarely black and white because they cannot be written to cover every conceivable situation.

My advice is to take advantage of what tax benefits you can, but never structure your affairs in such a way that you are dependent on a tax benefit being available. There should always be a good reason other than a tax benefit as to why you take a particular action.

Take advantage of government tax incentives

From time to time most governments offer tax incentives or other incentives to encourage saving. These incentives are liable to change with changes in government and in economic policy, so take advantage of them while they are available.

In New Zealand, there are considerable tax gains to be had with KiwiSaver and with Portfolio Investment Entities (PIEs), particularly for people on the highest marginal tax rate. More information on KiwiSaver can be found on pages 227–30 and on PIEs on pages 222–23.

Invest in assets for high capital gain

Perhaps the simplest way to minimise tax on investments is to invest in assets that produce little or no income, and large capital gain. These include shares, managed equity funds and undeveloped land.

This is because in many circumstances in New Zealand capital gain is not taxable. A note of caution though: to avoid tax, you will need to be able to prove that when you purchased the asset your intention was retain it for long-term benefit, rather than sell it for a quick capital gain.

In New Zealand, a property trader – someone who buys and sells several properties a year – will incur tax on the profit made. However, someone who buys a property to live in, makes improvements to it, and sells it some time later for a large gain will not normally be taxed on that gain.

> If you are willing to put in the effort, endure the chaos and move often, renovating a succession of houses in which you live can be a good way to grow your wealth.

Make use of tax-paid and tax-effective investments

Another way of minimising tax is to make use of tax-paid investments, such as insurance bonds and traded endowment policies. Income from tax-paid investments does not need to be included in your income tax return. Property and businesses are also tax-effective investments because you can claim interest, depreciation and other expenses against your income.

Structure ownership to attract tax benefits

Ownership of income-producing investments should be structured in a tax-effective manner.

Partner with lower tax rate

If a couple are on different marginal tax rates, it is obviously tax-effective for investments to be owned by the partner on the lower tax rate. However, consideration needs to be given to the implications of relationship property legislation, estate planning and gift duty. Giving your partner money to invest in their name because they are on a lower tax rate can incur gift duty. It can also mean that if your partner dies the investments will become part of their estate, and will be dealt with in accordance with their will.

Money given to a partner is also likely to be deemed relationship property, and will be dealt with as such under the law if your relationship ends. In New Zealand, the principal law governing relationship property is the Property (Relationships) Act.

Family trusts

A family trust can be advantageous in that trusts are taxed at a lower rate than the highest marginal tax rate for individuals. In New Zealand, trust income can either be taxed in the trust – at the trust tax rate – or distributed to beneficiaries, who then pay tax on it at their personal rates. In this way, trusts can be used to direct income towards adult beneficiaries (that is, those over the age of 16) who are on a low tax rate.

However, setting up a trust for the *sole purpose* of reducing tax can be deemed to be tax avoidance, so treat the tax savings from a trust as a bonus, rather than as the reason for setting it up.

Limited liability company

If you are self-employed, operating as a sole trader or partnership, and paying the highest rate of marginal tax, consider operating as a limited liability company.

In New Zealand, company tax is a flat rate, and lower than the highest rate of marginal tax for an individual. If you are a limited liability company, you can pay yourself a salary up to the level where your marginal tax rate is no higher than the company tax rate, and the company will pay tax on any additional income. You must ensure that you pay yourself a salary commensurate with your qualifications and experience. Paying yourself a salary of, say, $60,000 when the market salary for an equivalent role is $150,000 could be deemed to be tax avoidance.

With a company structure, you can also structure the shareholding so that the majority of shares are owned by the person with the lowest tax rate.

Each of these ownership structures has advantages and disadvantages, and you should always seek advice from an accountant and solicitor.

Minimising tax is just one consideration: it's important to look at the total impact each structure would have, including the cost of establishing and maintaining it, and the implications for estate planning and relationship property.

Tips for increasing income

HOARDER

Your challenge is to believe that you can earn more than you are now and deserve to do so. Here are my suggestions.

- Take the brakes off your thinking.
- Apply for a promotion or a new job.
- Acquire new skills that will lead to a pay rise.

ACHIEVER

As an achiever, you strive for success and status in your chosen career, and are probably already making the most of opportunities to earn more.

- Look at ways to reduce the amount of tax you pay.
- Actively seek out ways to get income outside your regular job – through investing in property, for example.

ENTREPRENEUR

You have no shortage of ideas for making millions.

- Sift through the opportunities, and focus on the one or two about which you feel most passionate.
- Look at ways of reducing the amount of tax you pay.

THRILL-SEEKER

You need to shift your focus from spending to earning.

- Find additional ways of earning money over and above your employment income. This extra income will help you pay off debt and create a surplus that you can invest.
- As you're not afraid to take risks, try setting up a small business you can operate from home in your spare time.

Use technology to create wealth automatically

Keeping track of personal income and expenditure is something even experts struggle with, and that includes accountants, bankers – and financial advisers. When you have a family to take care of, and you and your partner are both building careers, it is common for money to be left to look after itself.

That's when things get out of control. However large your income, by pay-day there never seems to be any money left, and it's a mystery where it has disappeared to. Setting up computer spreadsheets or using software packages to try and figure this out is like shutting the proverbial stable door after the horse has bolted.

Here's a typical household:

- Salaries and wages are paid into a joint bank account.
- Mortgage repayments, household expenses and personal expenses are deducted from this account.
- From time to time the account goes into overdraft, particularly if there is more than one Eftpos card or cheque book attached to it.
- Holidays and Christmas presents are paid for with a credit card, for which minimum repayments are made and the balance increases over time.
- Saving for retirement is non-existent.

> Money needs to be managed, and amazingly much of this can be done automatically, using direct debits, automatic payments and internet banking.

THRILL-SEEKERS AND ENTREPRENEURS

You will benefit most from a money-management system. Thrill-seekers often have no idea where their money goes, just that it has gone. Entrepreneurs are inclined to manage their financial affairs more on gut feeling than analysis.

HOARDERS AND ACHIEVERS

You will have no trouble managing your money in an organised way. Hoarders keep a close eye on where their money goes, and achievers are usually keen to keep track of their finances so they can see how their wealth is growing.

How to establish a money-management system

It is much easier to manage your money when it is divided up into several small accounts, rather than one big one. First, set a budget in which your income is divided into these key components:

long-term saving

medium-term saving

daily living expenses.

Next, divide your daily living expenses into:

fixed household expenses

semi-fixed household expenses

discretionary expenses.

Remember the Savings Equation:

Income =
daily living expenses + medium-term savings + long-term savings

There's an important principle that I call 'Pay yourself first'. Most people are quite good at paying bills to other people on time, but neglect their obligation to themselves, which is to set aside funds for the future. 'Pay yourself first' means putting your future needs at the top of your priority list.

When you set up a system for managing your money based on 'Pay yourself first', you reverse the order in which your money is used. In other words, the Savings Equation becomes:

Net income =
long-term savings + medium-term savings + daily living expenses.

Here's how to go about it.

1. **First, set up a deduction from your income for long-term savings – to cover your long-term working-life and retirement goals.** If you have already joined KiwiSaver or another employer-subsidised superannuation scheme, these contributions will be deducted directly from your pay.

   For additional savings – over and above your employer-subsidised scheme – set up a regular direct debit from your bank account each pay-day or each month to a diversified portfolio, diversified managed fund or superannuation scheme of the amount you have calculated you need to save each year in order to achieve your long-term goals.

   If you have a mortgage on your family home and have decided to delay long-term saving until it's paid off, your additional long-term savings should take the form of increased repayments on your mortgage.

2. **Next, set up a regular direct debit into an account for medium-term savings.** The amount should cover medium-term working-life goals and your emergency fund. It should be saved into an interest-bearing account that is readily accessible.

The amount left over after making these deductions is what you will have for everyday spending. In other words:

Daily living expenses =
net income – long-term savings and medium-term savings.

If you can keep your daily living expenses within this limit, you will be able to create sufficient wealth to achieve your working-life and retirement goals.

Managing daily living expenses

Interestingly, our grandparents seem to have managed their money a lot better than we do. Before the advent of electronic banking and when employees were typically paid in cash, money management was much simpler. Dad took out money for his beer and cigarettes, paid the rent or mortgage, and gave Mum the housekeeping money. Mum divided this into portions to cover food, clothes for the children, power, telephone, and perhaps (if there was any spare) new clothes for her and her husband, often putting each amount in a separate container. Because everything was done in cash, Mum and Dad always knew exactly how much money they had left until the next pay-day.

The secret to getting daily living expenses under control is to follow the same simple rules.

Rule 1 – *Have one manager for each of your bank accounts.*
Managing money is no different to managing anything else: the job should be given to one person, not two. This doesn't mean only one person should manage all the family finances, or that you shouldn't have joint accounts. It means that responsibilities should be divided between partners, with each partner being solely accountable for their chosen area or account.

For this to work, good communication is vital. For example, if your partner is the manager for your joint household expenditure account, you need to let him or her know when you have made transactions on that account.

Should couples keep their finances separate?

Some couples choose to keep their financial affairs completely separate. The main advantage is that both partners assume responsibility for meeting financial commitments, and learn how to manage money. When a relationship ends through death, separation or divorce, this can be an advantage.

There are several ways to manage joint expenses.

- Each partner pays 50% of each household bill. This can require a complicated accounting system to work out who owes what to whom.
- One partner gives the other a set amount each pay period to cover joint expenses. This system can sometimes leave the partner receiving the contribution feeling as though they are paying more than the other.
- Each partner contributes a set amount each pay period into a joint account from which household expenses are paid.
- Each partner agrees to take responsibility for certain payments. For example, one may pay the rates, power and phone, while the other pays for all the food.

However, if you have been together for three years or more, even if you are not married, don't assume that because you have managed your money separately you can walk away with your own savings in the event of a separation. In New Zealand, unless you have a formal agreement with your partner that states otherwise, under the provisions of the Property (Relationships) Act your savings, and even your personal superannuation, can be considered to be relationship property and split equally.

The main disadvantage of separating your financial affairs is that you are likely to end up with twice as many bank accounts as you need. Whether you choose to pool everything or keep it separate, don't make your money-management system too complicated. The simpler it is, the easier it will be to manage. Don't have too few accounts, but don't have too many either.

Rule 2 – ***Separate personal spending from household spending.***

How often have you run out of funds in your joint account because your partner has made a purchase or withdrawal and forgotten to tell you about it? Commonly, this situation arises because of personal spending.

It is obviously important for you to be able to spend money within agreed limits without consulting your partner. Each of you should, therefore, have your own personal account into which an agreed amount is siphoned each pay-day. This will set a limit on personal spending, but it will also give you freedom to spend money without being accountable to the other person.

These personal accounts should be clearly separated from accounts that are used for household expenditure.

Rule 3 – ***Separate known payments from variable payments.***

Another problem is that those direct-debits can catch you unawares. Just when you think your bank balance is looking healthy, along comes an insurance direct-debit or mortgage repayment you have forgotten was due.

These days it is quite common for half or two-thirds of income to be accounted for by direct-debits and automatic payments. The annoying thing is that the deductions are often monthly, whereas pay periods are fortnightly.

Big one-off payments such as car registration, school fees and club membership fees can also catch you off guard if you haven't set money aside for them.

In your budgeting, separate known payments from variable ones.

Known payment: You know the amount and the date of the payment with certainty.

Variable payment: You do not know the amount and/or the date of payment.

Known payments are usually unavoidable financial commitments. I recommend you set up all these payments to come out of one account, and variable ones to come out of another. This way you will have control, and avoid dishonour fees on direct-debits and automatic payments that do not clear.

You will also be able to put a definite limit on the money available for variable expenses.

Rule 4 – *Don't spend more than you have.*
For each account, set spending limits and adhere to them. Once you start going over your limit, or 'borrowing' money from one account to top up another, alarm bells should sound: you are losing control of your money.

Rule 5 – *Monitor your cash withdrawals.*
Wherever possible, use electronic payment methods – Eftpos, credit card and on-line bill payment. This will give you a clear record of what you have spent, and where.

Cash should be used only for personal spending on small items. Having cash in your wallet can tempt you to spend it, so keep cash holdings to a minimum. Set a limit on how much cash you will spend every week and make only one withdrawal of that amount.

> When you make an Eftpos purchase and are asked if you would like 'cash out', your answer should always be no – unless there is an extremely good reason to say yes.

Rule 6 – *Check your bank balances regularly.*
How often have you made a purchase without knowing if you have enough money to cover it? If you cross your fingers every time you use Eftpos in case the transaction gets declined, you are a poor money manager. This is a typical trait of a thrill-seeker.

You should know approximately how much money you have in each of your accounts at any time. With on-line banking and phone banking it is very easy to check your balances, and good money managers do this every few days.

There is a saying in management circles: 'What gets measured gets done'. If you want to improve the performance of your employees, you need to measure how well they're doing. The same principle applies to money. Checking your bank balances regularly will tell you how well you are managing your finances.

The 4x4 budget for daily living expenses

Most budgets fail because they take too much time to set up, and prove too complicated and time-consuming to monitor. When it comes to setting up your money-management system, you will find that daily living expenses present the biggest challenge. Wouldn't it be great to have a simple system that requires virtually no time and effort?

Right, forget about making lists of everything you spend money on. (This is good news for big-spending achievers and thrill-seekers.) Don't bother tracking every last dollar. Throw away those complicated spreadsheets, and the notebooks for recording all your purchases. Managing your money at such a detailed level does not work. Instead, implement the 4x4 budget.

> I guarantee it's the easiest, most effective budgeting system you will ever find, involving only four budget items and four simple steps.

These are the only four items you need in your budget:

your total known expenses

personal spending money for you

personal spending money for your partner

total variable household expenses.

Follow these four simple steps to set up your annual budgeting system.

Step 1 – *Identify your known expenses*

Go back to your budget sheet for daily living expenses. Identify and add up all known expenses over the course of a year – mortgage or rent, rates, insurance, car registration, school fees, club membership fees, gym membership fees, and so on. Remember, we are working only with living expenses, so don't include any savings at this stage.

Your fixed expenses will be known expenses, but so will some of your discretionary expenses – you may have decided to join a gym, subscribe to a magazine or go to a movie once a week, so these become known expenses.

Known expenses will all meet these two criteria:

- you know exactly how much you need to pay
- you know when you need to pay it.

Set aside a regular amount every pay-day to cover these expenses. After that, apart from occasional adjustments when charges change, you can forget about all those items.

> You have just dealt with around half your total budget.

Step 2 – *Agree on personal spending*

Now agree on an amount that you and your partner will each set aside each pay-day for personal discretionary expenses. These amounts don't need to be equal, but they do need to be mutually agreed to!

Step 3 – *Calculate your variable household spending*

Subtract your known expenses and personal spending money from the total amount of income you have allocated for daily living expenses. This is the amount you have left to cover your variable household living expenses such as food, power and phone. Do a quick cross-check to see if it's enough to live on. If it's not, you will need to cut back on your known expenses or personal spending money.

Step 4 – *Set up your bank accounts*

Allocate a different bank account to each of your four categories:

- personal account – you
- personal account – your partner
- known expenses account
- variable household expenses account.

Arrange to have your income paid into your principal account, which will be either your known expenses account or your variable household expenses account.

Next, divide your annual amount by the number of pay-days in the year – to convert your annual budget to a per-pay-day budget. Then arrange to transfer a fixed amount per pay period to each of the three other accounts. This can be readily set up on-line or through phone banking.

Here's an example of how this works, using 'known expenses' as the principal account.

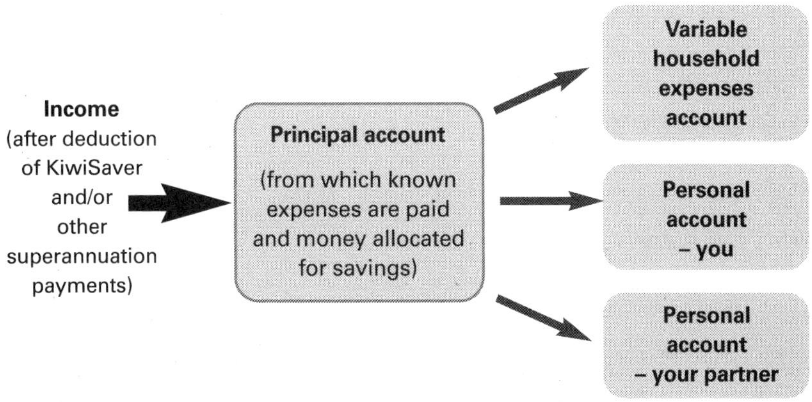

Now instead of trying to manage one big pool of money, you have four accounts – of which three manage themselves! You have substantially reduced the size of your problem. You have only one pool of money to worry about, and it will not get hit by as many unexpected items.

> The key to making this system work is keeping the spending in each account within the limits you have set.

If your 'personal expense' account runs out two days before pay-day, tough.

Your 'known expenses' account should automatically remain in balance if you have done your calculations correctly.

The 'variable household expenses' account will require the most effort to keep under control, but this will be a lot easier than managing all your income and expenditure from one account.

Your only remaining problem will be dealing with truly unplanned spending, such as car repairs and medical or dental expenses. Good news – you can pay for these from your emergency fund, which is part of your medium-term saving account.

While there may be additional bank fees for setting up the extra bank accounts, you will quickly find that the benefits – including increased saving – that come from this simple money management system far outweigh the costs.

Calculate your living expenses

	Expenditure	Fortnightly or monthly $	Annual total
Known expenses			
	Rates		
	Insurance (house, vehicles, personal)		
	Mortgage repayments		
	Loan repayments and hire purchase		
	Vehicle registration		
	Childcare – regular		
	Children's pocket money		
	School fees		
	Other		
	Sub-total		
Variable household expenses			
	Food		
	Power and fuel		
	Telephone		
	Transport		
	Childcare – occasional		
	Car maintenance		
	Medical and dental		
	Children's clothing and footwear		
	Other		
	Sub-total		
Personal expenses – you			
	Gifts		
	Haircuts		
	Clothing and footwear		
	Entertainment (including eating out)		
	Other		
	Sub-total		
Personal expenses – your partner			
	Gifts		
	Haircuts		
	Clothing and footwear		
	Entertainment (including eating out)		
	Other		
	Sub-total		
	Total daily living expenses		

Record your expenditure to establish how much you need to allocate to each spending category. Your total daily living expenses should equal your total income less the amount allocated to your long-term and medium-term saving plans.

Your total money-management system

Having done the budget for daily living expenses, you can now go back to the Savings Equation and add in long-term and medium-term savings.

In the table below, write down your net after-tax income per fortnight or per month, and into which account this money will be paid. Now, enter how much of this income you will save for your retirement, how much you will save for spending, and how much you will retain for living expenses – taking the information from the Savings Planner on page 108.

Then write down the name of the account in which you will keep this money. Your savings may go to more than one account. For example, you may have some going into a 'debt' account, or you may have more than one investment account.

Keep adjusting your goals and your budget until you achieve the right balance between long-term saving, saving for lifestyle, and paying for everyday living expenses.

	Account name	$ fortnightly	Sub-Total	Total
INCOME				
After-tax income – you				
After-tax income – your partner				
TOTAL INCOME				
SAVINGS AND EXPENSES				
Long-term saving				
Medium-term saving				
Total savings				
Known expenses (direct-debits, automatic payments, fixed expenses)				
Variable household expenses				
Personal expenses – you				
Personal expenses – your partner				
Total living expenses				
TOTAL SAVINGS + LIVING EXPENSES				

CASE STUDY

Here's how Warren and Kay set up their total money-management system.

- All income is paid into their savings account.
- From there, there are automatic transfers to:
  (1) a diversified fund for long-term saving
  (2) a credit card to pay for household variable expenses
  (3) two personal accounts.
- The remaining money in the savings account covers automatic payments and direct-debits, with the surplus covering medium-term saving .

	Account name	$ fortnightly	Sub-Total	Total
INCOME				
After-tax income – Warren		$1,975		
After-tax income – Kay		$269		
TOTAL INCOME	**Savings account**			**$2,244**
SAVINGS AND EXPENSES				
Long-term saving	Diversified fund (paid from savings account)	$76		
Medium-term saving	Savings account	$263		
Total savings			**$339**	
Known expenses (direct-debits, automatic payments, fixed expenses)	Savings account	$1,240		
Variable household expenses	Credit card (paid off monthly from savings account)	$525		
Personal expenses – Warren	Personal Eftpos savings account (transferred from savings account)	$100		
Personal expenses – Kay	Personal Eftpos savings account (transferred from savings account)	$40		
Total living expenses			**$1,905**	
TOTAL SAVINGS + LIVING EXPENSES				**$2,244**

Setting up accounts for everyday spending

The way you set up your accounts will depend very much on your personal circumstances and whom you bank with. Banks are becoming more innovative in the area of total money management. If you have a good relationship with your bank, make an appointment with a customer services representative and get his or her help to set up the best money management system for you.

If you own a property or properties, one way of managing your everyday spending is to set up your accounts like this:

1. Establish a line of credit secured against your home.
2. Set a target balance for this line of credit for the next one to five years. After allowing for your agreed emergency fund, any funds in excess of the target can be treated as saving for lifestyle spending.
3. Pay all household income into your line of credit to minimise your interest costs.
4. Arrange for all known costs – such as automatic payments and direct debits – to be deducted from this account.
5. Use a credit card for all variable household expenses. Set a limit on of the amount you have budgeted for variable household expenses. Arrange for this credit card to be paid automatically from your line of credit every month before interest is payable.
6. Set up an Eftpos account for each partner, and arrange for the agreed amount to be transferred to this account every fortnight or month from your line of credit.

If you don't own a property, you may have the following arrangements:

1. Pay all household income into an interest-bearing savings account. Set a target balance for his account that includes saving for emergencies and for lifestyle expenses.
2. Arrange for all known costs – such as automatic payments and direct debits – to be deducted from this account.

3 Use a credit card for all variable household expenses. Set a credit limit on this card of the amount you have budgeted for variable household expenses.

4 Arrange for this credit card to be paid automatically from your savings account every month before interest is payable.

5 Set up an Eftpos account for each partner, and arrange for the agreed amount to be transferred to this account every fortnight or month from your savings account.

Experiment with a system and see if it suits you. It's easy to change once you know what works and what doesn't.

For practicality you may want to make slight changes to the accounts from which certain types of expenses are paid. For example, the person who mows your lawns may not accept a credit card, so you may have to add the lawn-mowing into your personal account and pay him or her in cash.

The main thing is to be very clear which items come out of which account, and not to switch money from one account to another to cover budget blow-outs.

The golden rules for setting up a money-management system

In setting up your system, remember the six golden rules of money management, and ensure your system follows them as far as practically possible.

1 Have one account manager for each bank account.

2 Separate personal spending from household spending.

3 Separate known payments from variable ones.

4 Don't spend more money than you have.

5 Monitor your cash withdrawals.

6 Check your bank balances regularly.

Multiply your money

We have looked at how to cut your expenditure and increase your net income, so you are in a position where your income is greater than your expenditure. In other words, you can save. Now let's look at how to go further and actually *create* wealth.

To create wealth, you can invest your own money that you have saved, or you can invest other people's money that you have borrowed.

Let's start by looking at how to use your own money. Here's what you should do to gain the greatest benefit from your savings:

- Join a subsidised superannuation scheme.
- Pay off short-term debt, such as credit-card and hire-purchase debt.
- Set aside money for short-term spending or emergencies.
- Buy your first house – either to live in or as an investment property.
- Pay off your mortgage.
- Set up a savings and investment portfolio.
- Reduce your risk.

Join a subsidised superannuation scheme

If you are looking for a good return on your money, it's hard to beat a superannuation scheme that offers subsidies or incentives. In New Zealand, KiwiSaver is an example of such a scheme, and many employers also offer their own schemes in which they make a matched contribution.

If, for example, you are contributing 4% of your pay to an employer scheme and your employer is also contributing 4%, in effect you are instantly doubling the value of each contribution you make. That's an immediate 100% return on your investment.

There are usually conditions attached to the schemes. For example, you may not be eligible for the full amount of the employer contribution if you withdraw your funds within a certain period, or your funds may be locked in until you reach a certain age.

Pay off short-term debt

It is important to build a solid foundation for your wealth-creation process. This means getting rid of debt and creating an emergency fund that will prevent you from going back into debt.

It's a reality of life that, with student loans, mortgages, car loans and credit-card spending, together with the expenses of raising a family, most of us will spend around half our lives in debt.

We are often told that we must start saving early, and consistently put aside a percentage of our income into a long-term investment fund. But does it make sense to save when you are in debt?

The first thing to consider is the cost of your debt. Your most expensive debt – the one with the highest rate of interest – will be your credit card. The rate of interest here could be around 20% per annum, so if you have a debt of $1,000 you will be paying $200 interest over the course of a year.

Your next most expensive debt will be unsecured personal loans (such as an overdraft), followed by secured loans (such as a car loan), and your mortgage.

Secondly, consider the rate of return you can expect to obtain on an investment. A rate of 10% over the long term is probably at the top limit of what you can achieve without taking on considerable risk.

Thirdly, have a look at your marginal tax rate. If you have $1,000 to invest and can get a return of 10%, you will receive a gross income of $100. Depending on your marginal tax rate, you will end up with a net $80.50 (assuming a 19.5% tax rate), $67.00 (assuming a 33% tax rate) or $61.00 (assuming a 39% tax rate).

Putting these three things together, the picture becomes clearer. With credit-card debt, if you keep it and invest the $1,000 you will have a cost of $200 and an offsetting income of between $61.00 and $80.50. It would obviously be best to repay the debt.

Even if you used low-cost mortgage debt at, say, 7.5% interest, you would need to earn between 9.3% and 12.3% gross on your investment, depending on your tax rate, to make investing worthwhile.

However, there are other factors which could alter the picture.

Your money personality

While it may be your best intention to start saving once your debts are paid, this isn't always what happens in practice. If you are not in the habit of saving, you may find it tempting to spend your spare cash rather than save it. This will be particularly true of achievers and thrill-seekers. There is a real danger that once your debts are paid off you incur more debt – for example, buying new furniture or a bigger house or going on an overseas trip. Setting up a savings scheme, even if you are only contributing a small amount each month, will get you into the savings habit and make it easy for you to simply increase your automatic payments into your savings account once the debt payments have ceased.

Penalty costs

If you have a fixed-interest rate on your mortgage, or an early repayment penalty on your personal loan, there may be penalty costs if you repay early.

Matching contributions

If you invest in a superannuation scheme where your contributions are matched by your employer and/or by a government contribution – for example KiwiSaver – you will make a higher return than if you repay debt.

Tax-deductibility

You may be able to make investing worthwhile if your debt costs can be made tax-deductible against your investment income, or if you can reduce the tax on your investment income by careful tax planning.

Create an emergency fund

Once you have cleared your short-term debt, creating an emergency fund will help you stay out of debt. An emergency fund can be used for unexpected expenses and to cover periods when your income might drop, such as if you are unable to work.

Your emergency fund should be kept in a call account or cash management fund, where the money can be accessed quickly, ideally within one to two days. Even though it is on call, it should be able to attract a good interest rate. Shop around before deciding where to place it. Funds for short-term spending (that is, within the next three to six months) can be added to your emergency fund.

Some banks are now offering a money-management system whereby funds held in a savings account can be offset against a mortgage balance, thus reducing the amount of interest you pay on your mortgage.

Line of credit

There is another alternative. Rather than holding emergency funds in a low interest-bearing account, you may choose to have a line of credit, which can be used in case of emergency, secured against your house by way of a mortgage. This way, you can invest all your funds for a longer time period at a higher rate of interest, yet still have access to money if you need it.

You will pay interest only on the funds that you draw down when the emergency arises, and the interest you pay should be offset by the interest you are earning on the funds that you have invested.

> You should have a line of credit only if you are disciplined enough not to use it for anything other than emergency purposes. Thrill-seekers beware!

Buy your first house

While the house in which you live is not, strictly speaking, an investment, purchasing a home is an important part of wealth-creation. High property prices can make it difficult for young couples or singles to buy a house, but most still dream of owning their own home, and having a pleasant environment in which to live and perhaps raise a family.

Before you consider buying a house, you need to be financially sound. Consider this checklist. Have you:

- ◯ Revised your budget so you are able to save?
- ◯ Paid off all short-term debt?
- ◯ Created an emergency fund?
- ◯ Saved enough of a deposit to make a mortgage manageable?

If the answer to all these questions is yes, you can feel confident about purchasing a house. If it's not, you should keep working towards it.

Stay cool

Buying a house is often as much about emotion as it is about money. It's easy to get emotionally attached to a house that is not affordable, and a natural human tendency to want something that's slightly out of reach. For this reason, some people make mistakes with their first home purchase.

Emotional attachment can also mean you pay a higher price because you are afraid of missing out. This is a real concern in an overheated market.

And impatience can lead to another mistake – not taking a long-term view. How will the mortgage be paid if and when there is only one income coming in? How will repairs, maintenance and upgrades be paid for? And what will happen if interest rates go up?

Where to start

There are four key steps to take before you buy a first home:

1. Establish some criteria for the kind of home that will best suit your needs – for example, size, proximity to transport and schools, and type of construction.
2. Have a look at some properties that meet those criteria to get a feel for how much you will have to pay.
3. Talk to your bank or mortgage broker about how much deposit you will need, how much you will be able to borrow, and what your fortnightly repayments will be. You will need to be in a strong

financial position before you buy, because once you are committed to a large mortgage it will be difficult to save.

4 Compare the rent you are currently paying with the cost of owning a house. This cost includes mortgage payments, rates and house repairs, such as plumbing, electrical and painting. You may be currently paying $300 per week in rent, but once you own a house you may be paying $600 per week in mortgage payments, rates and insurance.

> If the house you want to buy is truly affordable, you should be able to save the difference each week between what you currently pay in rent and what it will cost you to own the house.

Start saving that money now – *before* you buy the house – and put it towards the deposit. This will be a true test of whether you can afford to buy. And the higher your deposit the lower your repayments will be, giving you a bit more leeway to cover interest rate increases or a drop in income.

Your first home doesn't need to be a big family home that is going to last you for 20 years. Start with something small and affordable and work your way up. Being forced to sell because you can't manage the mortgage would cost you a lot of money.

Some people start out by buying an investment property. It can be easier to find a house that is affordable if you are not going to live in it yourself, because you can consider buying in areas other than where you would choose to live. Expenses such as interest, rates, repairs and depreciation will also be tax-deductible, making the purchase much more affordable.

Alternatively, you may choose to live in the house yourself but take in boarders or flatmates to help with the rent.

Through most of your life your home will probably be your biggest asset, and the choice you make with your first purchase will have a significant impact on your future wealth. It's worth doing your homework to avoid making a costly mistake.

Pay off your mortgage

The sooner you can pay off your mortgage, the quicker you will be able to multiply your wealth. To find out how long it will take you to repay your mortgage, or how large your repayments will need to be if you are to pay it off within a certain period of time, use a mortgage repayment calculator. Some banks have this on their websites, and there is also one at *www.sorted.org.nz*.

Here's an example. You have a mortgage of $100,000 at 9% interest, and you want to pay it off within 10 years. The fortnightly repayments will be $584.66. Alternatively, if you able to pay off only $500 per fortnight, it will take you 13 years and 2 months to repay the mortgage.

How to pay off your mortgage faster

1. Instead of repaying at the contracted amount, try setting your repayment amount a little higher. For example, if you have a 20-year mortgage requiring repayments of $1,000 per month, set your repayments at $1,100 per month, or whatever amount the bank will allow you to repay without incurring an early repayment penalty. If you find it difficult to keep up the higher repayments, you can always drop them back down to $1,000. It is better to do it this way around than to contract to pay the mortgage back at $1,100 per month, and then find that you can't keep up the repayments.
2. Make fortnightly, rather than monthly, repayments. For example, if you have a mortgage of $250,000 at 8.5% interest, paying it off at $2,000 per month will take you around 25 years and 7 months. If instead you make repayments of $1,000 per fortnight, you will be free of your mortgage in 20 years and 1 month. That's a saving of five and a half years and $132,000.

Set up a savings and investment portfolio

If we have children, it is generally not until we are in our forties or fifties and they have left home that we can think about approaching that blissful state of being debt-free. That's when the panic sets in. We suddenly realise how little time there is (usually calculated in pay-days rather than months or years) until we retire, and how little we have saved.

While it may, in theory, be better to repay all debt and then save like mad, not everyone will be disciplined enough to do this. Thrill-seekers and achievers, having reduced or paid off debt, may be inclined to keep spending on a bigger or better house, a new car or an overseas trip. They may even get back into debt.

If this is your problem, you need to develop a savings habit. Set aside a small amount each month and put it into an investment where the funds are not easily accessible. While the balance will at first seem to grow slowly, the power of compounding will soon generate a decent-sized nest egg.

The way you set up an investment portfolio will depend on:

- your money personality
- your investment time frame
- the goals you wish to achieve
- whether you require income or growth from your portfolio, or both
- how much you have to invest, whether as a lump sum or regular monthly savings.

Start the process by separating out your medium-term and long-term needs.

Saving and investing for medium-term spending

If you plan to set aside funds for spending within, say, a five-year time frame, whatever your money personality you should put them into an investment that has a reasonable return, a stable capital value, and a reasonable degree of liquidity – that is, you can get your money back when it suits you, rather than having it locked in.

This usually means putting the money into a cash management fund, and/or fixed-interest investments such as bank deposits, finance company debentures or bonds. These investments will provide income, which can be compounded, but the capital value will not fluctuate in value (other than through the additions that are made by compounding the interest).

If you invest money that you need in the medium term in volatile assets such as shares, you run the risk of having to sell those investments at a time when their value has dropped, rather than holding them until they regain their value.

Property is not suited for medium-term investing either, as it can be very illiquid: when you need the funds it may take months to find a buyer, and you may be forced to sell below market price. The exception is investment in property trusts that are listed on the stock exchange. In this case you can release your money by selling your shares.

Saving and investing for the long term

If you have time on your side, you can improve the rate of return on your money by investing in assets that change in capital value over time. Providing you have at least a five-year, and preferably a ten-year, time frame, you will be able to ride out the ups and downs.

You need to be able to have your funds invested for as long as it takes for the investment to achieve a good rate of return, so the point at which you sell will ultimately be determined by the investment markets, rather than your need for cash. This is called 'investing for growth', and comes from only two types of investment:

- business – either your own business, or (by buying shares) somebody else's
- property.

Putting all or most of your investment funds into growth assets carries both a potentially high return and a high degree of risk. If you are an entrepreneur or a thrill-seeker, this won't be a problem, but if you are a hoarder or an achiever you will want to lessen the risk by including cash and fixed-interest investments in your portfolio.

Investment principles

Investing is not rocket science. There are four types of asset in which you can invest.

Cash – for example bank deposits and cash-management funds.

Fixed interest – for example bank term-deposits, finance company debentures, bonds and government stock.

Property – for example listed property trusts, and commercial or residential property.

Shares – either in listed public companies or in your own business.

With each of these you have a choice as to whether you invest locally or offshore, although cash holdings are usually local.

Each type of asset has a different role to play in an investment portfolio.

Cash provides liquidity (in other words, you can get easy access to it), and a small return. At times when investment markets are volatile or expected to underperform, it makes sense to hold more cash than usual in your portfolio.

Fixed-interest investments provide certainty of capital value, and a regular income stream that can be compounded if necessary. An investment portfolio based largely on fixed-interest investments will grow in value consistently but slowly. Fixed-interest investments do, however, tend to be eroded over time by tax and inflation.

Shares provide a small income stream by way of dividends, and the opportunity to make a capital gain over the long term. However, they are volatile in value. The share market moves in cycles several years long, and to make a good capital gain it is usually necessary to hold shares through two or more cycles

Setting up your own business carries the potential to make good capital gain, but also the risk that your business may fail.

Property offers both a good income stream and the opportunity to make a capital gain. The property market also moves in cycles, but it is less volatile than the share market. While the house in which you live is not an investment as such, buying your own home is an important part of the wealth-creation process.

Risk and return

Risk and return go together. Each of the four asset classes has a different 'risk and return' profile.

Cash has the lowest risk and the lowest return.

Fixed interest has a higher risk than cash and a slightly higher return.

Shares have the highest potential return but the highest risk.

Property sits between fixed interest and shares.

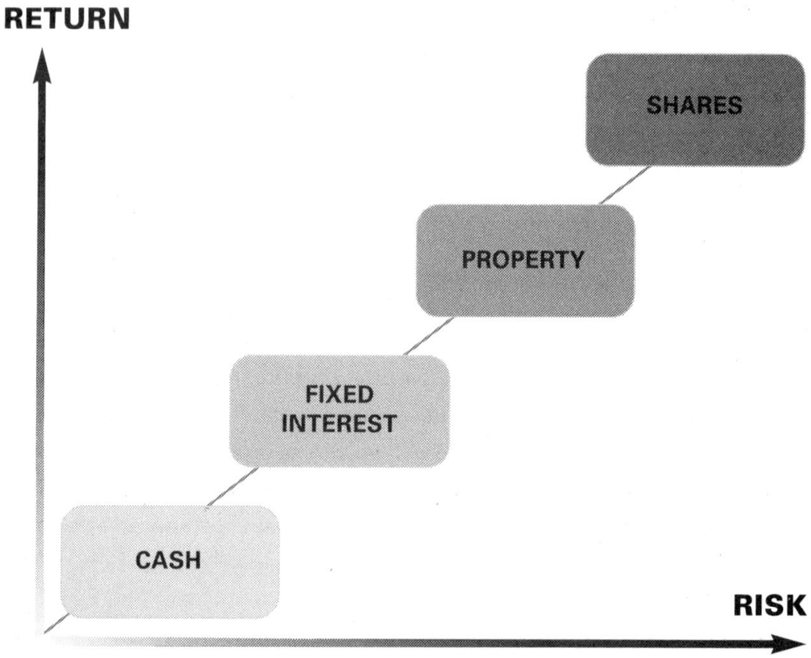

The level of risk you take on will depend on your money personality.

ENTREPRENEUR AND **THRILL-SEEKER**

You are natural risk-takers, and will feel comfortable with strategies such as property investment and share investment. Your challenge will be to ensure that you don't put *all* your assets or income at risk. Some of your existing wealth should be invested for security, so that both your long-term retirement needs and any short-term and medium-term planned expenditure can be accommodated.

HOARDER AND **ACHIEVER**

You will find it difficult to multiply your wealth because of your natural aversion to taking risks. Your challenge will be to try and obtain a better return on your investments while still taking an acceptable level of risk. Some of your existing wealth should be invested for growth so your long-term retirement needs are achievable.

Reduce your risk

For investment purposes, risk is defined as the chance that an investment will not perform as you expect. It means that you might not get your money back and you might not get any additional returns, such as interest, dividends or capital gain.

Here's how to reduce your investment risk.

Diversify

Diversification is the key to wise investing. It enables you to maximise the return on your investments, while keeping risk to a comfortable level. Buy smaller quantities of many different investments, rather than having all your eggs in one basket. Invest in different asset classes, different geographic areas and different companies. A diversified investment portfolio will have investments in each of the asset classes.

Invest for the long term

If you put money in risky assets, plan to do so for a long time – that is, leave your investment in place until it reaches a satisfactory value.

Fixed-interest investment

One of the biggest risks of a fixed-interest investment is that you will lose your interest and/or capital through the borrower being unable to make interest payments or repay the amount you have invested. You must be careful not to chase high returns without being fully aware of the risks involved in achieving those returns.

The credit crisis of 2007, which resulted in losses in fixed-interest investments such as fixed-interest funds and finance companies, is a reminder of this. For long-term investment, it pays to invest in quality assets that produce an adequate return, rather than higher-returning assets that have a high risk of loss.

Many fixed-interest investments now have a credit rating, and this is a good indication of how likely the company is to default on payments.

> Always study a company's credit rating before investing.

The three dominant rating bodies are Standard and Poor's, Moody's and Fitch. Before these organisations give a rating, they do a thorough analysis of the company offering the investment. As well as looking at its financial performance, they consider the quality of its management and internal processes, along with many other factors that may have an impact on the company's success or failure.

Each rating organisation has a different scale, and you need to understand how the scale works to understand whether a particular rating is good or bad. Standard and Poor's uses the scale at the top of the next page.

This means, for example, that of 100 companies with a rating of BB, less than two are likely to default within a one-year period, but on average nine will default over a five-year period.

These ratings can be further modified by the addition of a + or –. An investment that is rated BBB– or above is considered to be investment grade, with an AAA rating being extremely strong, and a C rating being highly vulnerable.

Standard and Poor's rating system

Rating	Estimated probability of default over one-year period	over five-year period (cumulative average)
AAA	0–0.01%	0.29%
AA	0.01–0.02%	0.21%
A	0.05–0.1%	0.63%
BBB	0.2–0.4%	2.14%
BB	0.6–1.6%	9.02%
B	3.0–11.0%	25.77%
CCC, CC and C	25–30%	46.22%

Source: www.yourinvestments.standardandpoors.co.nz

Another risk is that interest rates will change. The longer the period for which you fix the rate, the more likely it is that this will happen. An interest rate of 9% for five years may seem attractive now, but it won't look so flash if interest rates rise to 11% next year.

Set up your fixed-interest investments to mature at different times. If they mature together, you may have to reinvest them all when interest rates are low.

Reduce the risk of fixed-interest investment

- Ask for the credit rating of each company, bank or specific investment (for example, bond or note) in which you are considering placing funds.
- Spread your money among several different companies or banks.
- If interest rates are rising, don't invest for too long a term.
- Spread the maturities of your investments, so all your funds won't be reinvested at the same time.

Share investment

The risk of investing in shares is slightly different. The risk of losing your capital is dependent not only on the performance of the companies in which you invest, but on cyclical movements in the share market, and the length of time for which the funds are invested.

Reduce the risk of a share portfolio

- Diversify your portfolio by geographic area, type of industry and size of company. Small or medium-sized companies often perform better than large ones.
- Be prepared to leave your funds invested for as long as it takes to ride through market fluctuations. This may be ten years or longer.
- Don't panic when the market falls. Remember that markets are cyclical. Falling markets are always followed by rising markets, and the best time to buy is when prices are down.

Business ownership

For tips on how to reduce risk with your own business, see pages 250–59.

Property investment

Contrary to popular perception, property does not always rise in value. However, property values fluctuate in cycles, and as most people hold property for some time before selling it they don't notice the various changes in value between purchase and sale.

The return from investment property consists of income (rent or lease payments) and/or capital gain. An oversupply of rental property forces down both rents and property values. There is a risk of rent increasing by a smaller percentage than property prices, thus lowering the yield (income divided by property value) on property over time.

There is also a risk that your income will be lowered through vacancies, or tenants defaulting on payments. As with shares, property is best viewed as a long-term investment.

Reduce the risk of property investment

- Diversify your portfolio so it contains both properties that promise high capital gain and those that offer a good income yield.
- Look for ways of improving the yield – for example, make small improvements to the property that lead to a higher rent, as well as a higher capital value.
- Be careful to select properties that will attract good tenants.
- Learn how to select tenants who can afford to pay the rent – for example, by using credit checks and references.
- Before you buy, calculate your expected cash flow so you know how much of your own money, if any, will be required to service the mortgage.

Investment risk and return

One way to test your money personality is to imagine what you would do if you were to win $500,000 in a lottery.

If you are a **hoarder**, your first inclination will be to tuck your windfall safely in the bank, where you can keep a close eye on it and watch it grow, albeit slowly.

Thrill-seekers will be inclined to spend most of it on things that have little or no lasting value, such as holidays, clothes and entertainment.

Achievers will probably decide to extend and renovate their house, buy a new car or two, and perhaps squeeze in a couple of overseas trips.

If there is anything left over, thrill-seekers and achievers will generally see the benefits of diversifying their investments with a mix of different asset classes. But their biggest challenge will be to invest, rather than spend.

Entrepreneurs will view the cash windfall as an opportunity to make even more money through investing in growth assets, such as property and shares, or setting up a business – even if the venture carries a high degree of risk.

Only two money personality types, hoarders and entrepreneurs, are truly investors by nature.

Tips for investing

HOARDER

Hoarders are comfortable only with safe, secure investments, and are therefore willing to accept a low rate of return. If you are a hoarder, the thought of investing in shares will be rather scary: hoarders are primarily cash and fixed-interest investors.

Your biggest investment challenge is to diversify your portfolio into assets with which you would normally not be comfortable, in order to improve your return.

- Use time to your advantage. Market volatility is the biggest component of risk for investments in growth assets such as property and shares. The longer your investment time frame, the less your risk will be because markets are less volatile over the long term.

  Set aside a small part of your portfolio to which you won't need access for the next ten years or so, and use it to invest in property or shares.

- Reduce your risk and increase your peace of mind by getting advice from an expert.

ENTREPRENEUR

Entrepreneurs value the potential for high returns above security. If you are an entrepreneur, you believe that you can pick opportunities and you aren't afraid to have all your eggs in one basket. You don't believe in diversification of your investments because you consider this will lower your return. Your biggest challenge will be to diversify your portfolio into assets which you would normally consider to be too mundane.

- Set aside part of your portfolio to be invested in lower risk investments (for example, fixed interest) for security rather than return.
- As you make profits on your ventures, set part of your profit aside in safe investments.

ACHIEVER

Achievers prefer to spend their money on things that improve their current lifestyle or status, rather than investing so as to have a higher standard of living in the future. They also have a lower willingness to take risks than an entrepreneur or thrill-seeker. If you are an achiever, your biggest challenge will be to invest, rather than spend.

- Set up a regular savings scheme to build up funds for investment.
- Consider borrowing to invest, for example in property, but within limits to suit your conservative nature.

THRILL-SEEKER

Thrill-seekers are more likely than any other personality type to be struggling with debt, and it won't make sense to invest until the debts are gone. As a thrill-seeker, you can take advantage of your willingness to take risk by getting your thrills from potentially high returning investments rather than shopping sprees.

- Start taking life a bit more seriously by getting rid of your debt and setting up a regular savings scheme to build up funds for investment.
- Channel your willingness to take risks into investment opportunities that will help grow your wealth

How to get rich fast

If you want your wealth to increase in leaps and bounds rather than small steps, only three types of investment can achieve this:

- your own business
- shares
- property

These are referred to as 'growth assets'. Investing for growth means accepting a high level of risk.

How to allocate your investment money

Whether you are investing a lump sum or regular small amounts of savings, the same principles apply. How you divide your investment portfolio among the asset classes – cash, fixed-interest, property and shares – is what financial planners call 'asset allocation'.

The asset allocation should also show how your portfolio is split between onshore and offshore investments.

Now answer these questions.

- ◯ Are you a hoarder or achiever?
- ◯ Do you have a relatively short investment time frame – say five years or less?
- ◯ Do you need income from your investments?

If the answer to each question is yes, your portfolio should focus on cash and fixed-interest investments.

A hoarder who is retired or working less, and wants to receive a steady income from his or her investments may have this asset allocation:

Asset class	Onshore %	Offshore %	Total
Cash	15	0	15
Fixed-interest	45	15	60
Property	5	0	5
Shares	5	15	20
Total	**70**	**30**	**100**

Here's another set of questions.

- ◯ Are you an entrepreneur or a thrill-seeker?
- ◯ Do you have a relatively long investment time frame – five years or more?
- ◯ Do you want to significantly grow the value of your portfolio to achieve your goals, even at the expense of income?

If the answer to each is yes, your portfolio should be more heavily weighted to growth assets, such as shares and property.

An asset allocation for an entrepreneur who wants to achieve substantial investment growth may look like this:

Asset class	Onshore %	Offshore %	Total
Cash	5	0	5
Fixed-interest	10	5	15
Property	15	0	15
Shares	20	45	65
Total	**50**	**50**	**100**

While your asset allocation can be changed over time, you need to bear in mind that your share portfolio will fluctuate in value, and once you have purchased shares you may be committed to them until the required return has been achieved.

It is, therefore, extremely important to get the asset allocation right *before* you begin investing. If it is not set correctly, you will either have more volatility in your portfolio than you are comfortable with (if the share allocation is too high), or your portfolio will not grow as quickly as you want it to (if the fixed-interest allocation is too high).

Growth portfolios will usually be highly volatile in the short term, while stable portfolios will usually show low growth over the long term.

> The most important investment decision you will ever make is your asset allocation. At least 80% of the return you achieve will be determined by the split.

CASE STUDY

Graham and Gail, a couple in their fifties, came to see me with two portfolios – one for themselves and one for Graham's mother. Graham had a job where a house was provided, and rather than rent out their family home they had decided to sell it, invest the money and purchase again in two to three years' time when Graham retired. Graham's mother, aged in her eighties, was living in a rest-home; the return on her portfolio was helping pay for her care.

The advice Graham had been given on the two substantial portfolios was to invest over 90% in shares, mostly international. This was at a time when the international share market was showing returns of 15% to 25% per annum. Of course, the inevitable happened. Shortly after they invested, the international share market went into one of its biggest periods of decline in 100 years. The combined loss on the portfolios was well over $100,000.

Both of these portfolios should have been largely in fixed-interest investments. The couple had a short investment time frame and needed to count on having the money available to purchase a house. Not only did they lose money on their shares, but house prices moved up sharply. They were now faced with taking on a mortgage, making do with a very basic home for their retirement, or working longer to try and recoup some of the capital they had lost.

Fixed-interest investments would also have provided a good income for Graham's mother, and preserved her capital for the benefit of her children. While there was enough capital to pay the rest-home fees, Graham and his siblings now faced receiving a greatly reduced inheritance.

CASE STUDY **ASSET ALLOCATION**

CASE STUDY

My clients Warren and Kay, whom I discussed on page 147, are aged 50. They have determined that to reach their goals they need to save the following:

	Annual saving required	**Number of years**
Emergency fund	$1,883	5
Working-life goals – medium-term (within the next five years)	$4,966 then dropping	5
Working-life goals – long-term (five years and more)	$1,997 then dropping	8–10
Retirement goals	$17,440	10, starting in 5 years' time

The asset allocation for the saving and investment required would be:

Goals	**Saving**	**Investment**
Emergency fund	Call account, or cash management fund	Call account, or cash management fund
Working-life goals – medium-term	Regular and lump sum contributions to a call account or cash management fund	Fixed-interest investments, such as term deposits, finance company debentures, and bonds
Lifetime goals – long-term – and retirement goals	Regular and lump sum contributions to a diversified fund	Diversified portfolio of cash (5%), fixed-interest (35%), property (5%), shares (55%)

CASE STUDY **ASSET ALLOCATION**

Long-term thinking

When setting your asset allocation, don't be concerned about the past performance of an asset class. All investments go through performance cycles, and trying to pick winners in the short term does not work. If anything, a sustained period of strong performance is often an indication that future performance is likely to drop.

That said, you should still invest in an asset class even if you expect its performance to drop in the short term. You will never be able to pick the best time: the important thing is to take the plunge and invest across all asset classes, then hold on until you have been through a few market cycles.

The principle of dollar-cost averaging

Saving a regular amount each month into an investment portfolio is a good way to build up assets, such as shares, that change in value over time. Purchasing small amounts regularly enables you to average out the price you pay, so you don't have to worry about when is the best time to invest.

If you invest a set amount of money on a regular basis over a long period of time, you will automatically buy less when the market is up and more when it is down. This is called dollar-cost averaging.

Of course, dollar-cost averaging does not guarantee a profit, but it can smooth out the market's ups and downs, and reduce the risk you run when investing in volatile markets.

Borrowing to invest

One of the most powerful techniques for building wealth quickly is to use leveraging. In simple terms, leveraging can be thought of as using other people's money instead of – or as well as – your own so as to increase your investing power.

The most common way of leveraging is to buy an investment property by taking out a mortgage. Here's how it works. You have $20,000 to invest. Obviously, you can't buy a house with $20,000, but you can use the

$20,000 as a deposit on a house worth $200,000 and borrow the remaining $180,000 at an interest rate of, say, 6%.

Let's say your investment property produces a gross return of 10% a year in rental income and capital gain – a total of $20,000 – and requires expenditure (on interest, rates, insurance and so on) of $15,000 a year. Your net return is therefore $5,000, which is an annual return of 25% on the original $20,000 you invested.

The reason this works is quite simple: the return achieved on the investment asset is higher than the cost of borrowing. But if it is that simple, why aren't there more wealthy people?

The reason is that leveraging is a double-edged sword. It is not always possible to establish beforehand whether the return on your investment asset will be greater than the cost of borrowing.

Sometimes, for example, interest rates will increase so much from what you were originally paying that you will start making a negative return. Instead of magnifying your gains you will magnify your losses. Going back to our example, if the gross return on the investment property is 6% or $12,000 and expenses are $15,000, your will lose $3,000, or 15% of your original investment.

> One of the advantages of leveraging is that if you borrow for the specific purpose of purchasing an income-producing asset, the interest is usually tax-deductible against the income.

While it is widely known that this tax-deductibility applies in the case of an investment property, and establishing or purchasing a business, it is not so commonly known that it also applies to other assets, such as shares and fixed-interest investments.

If, for example, you take out a mortgage on your home for the specific purpose of purchasing a share portfolio, the interest can be tax-deductible.

The share portfolio itself can also be used as security, but in this case the amount that can be borrowed will be limited to around 50% to 80%, depending on the specific investments in the portfolio. The lender will specify a borrowing percentage for each share against which they are willing to lend. This is known as *margin lending*.

Leveraged share portfolios are usually offered through the larger share-broking firms or specialist margin lenders. One of the benefits of margin lending is that it enables you to diversify your portfolio more than you would be able to by borrowing against existing investments to purchase additional shares. Alternatively, it allows you to access some of the funds you have invested in a portfolio without having to sell the investments.

Here's a simple example of how it works. Let's say you have $30,000 of your own money to invest in a share portfolio. Let's also assume that the margin lending ratio for each company in the portfolio is 70%, so you can buy $100,000 worth of shares. If the value of the portfolio increases by 10%, you will make $10,000 – a return of 33% on your capital of $30,000. In addition, there may be dividends payable.

However, from your total return (capital gain plus dividends) you will need to deduct brokerage and interest costs. The dividends can be used to cover some of the cost of borrowing, but it is likely you will need to make a monthly payment to cover the full cost of the debt, in the

Leveraging – give it a go!

The more certainty there is around the relationship between the investment return and the borrowing cost, the lower the risk that leveraging poses.

Before you embark on a leveraged investment, you should estimate the likely returns under a number of different scenarios: best case, worst case and expected. That way, there will be no surprises.

Once you have done your homework and the risks and return look reasonable, don't be afraid to proceed.

expectation that eventually the capital gain on the shares will be greater than the cost of the debt.

> The disadvantage of buying a leveraged share portfolio is that shares are volatile in value.

Depending on the agreement you have with the lender, if share values drop you may be forced to contribute more capital to keep the loan-to-value ratio within the agreed limits. You also run the risk of making an overall loss on the portfolio if, for any reason, you are forced to sell while the values are low.

Endowment warrants

Endowment warrants are another form of leveraged investment. An endowment warrant is an investment that gives you the right to purchase shares at a time in the future, based on their price today. You acquire the right to this future purchase by making an initial payment now – a fraction of the value of the shares – then a final payment when the warrants mature. This final amount will include accrued interest on the residual amount, less any dividends payable.

Endowment warrants can be sold prior to maturity, and at maturity you can choose to take either full ownership of the shares by paying the final amount, or an equivalent cash payment.

Leveraging and your money personality

Leveraging offers potentially high returns, but it also carries high risks. Whether it is appropriate for you depends on your money personality and your overall financial situation.

ENTREPRENEUR

You can use leveraging extensively as a way to increase wealth fast.

HOARDER

Leveraging will be out of your comfort zone, but you shouldn't be afraid to try it with the help of someone whose knowledge and experience you value.

ACHIEVER AND THRILL-SEEKER

You can use leveraging in moderation, but do your homework first.

Calculating your borrowing capacity

Before you commit to a leveraged investment, you will need to establish your borrowing capacity. It pays to meet with your bank before you sign any purchase agreements, so you can establish the level of borrowing they will approve.

Banks usually apply two tests to determine how much money they will lend you.

First, they look at the loan-to-value ratio – that is, the value of the total loan divided by the value of the assets (for example, the property) to be used as security. A different ratio will be used for different types of security, for example for commercial property, residential property or shares. For residential property your loan-to-value ratio will usually have to be 80% at most, although under certain circumstances it may be increased to 95%.

Secondly, the bank will look at the value of your monthly financial outgoings compared to your monthly total income (including rent, dividends and interest). Outgoings include mortgage payments, rent or board, hire-purchase payments, credit card minimum payments, other loan payments, child care fees, child support payments, and any other financial obligations. In order to secure a loan, these outgoings will normally need to be no more than 35% of your gross monthly income.

If you are borrowing to purchase a residential rental property, usually only 70% to 75% of the annual rent will be included in the income calculation, to allow for periods when the property will be vacant, or when tenants default on rent payments.

Managing your investment portfolio

There is no such thing as a 'set and forget' investment portfolio. To minimise your risk and increase your return, your portfolio must be managed – either by you or by someone you entrust with the task.

These tasks are important.

1 Regularly review and maintain the asset allocation – how is your portfolio divided among the different asset classes?

2 Occasionally review the specific investments *within* each asset class. How are they performing? Should anything be changed?

3 Keep good records of prices paid, income or distributions received, and changes in value over time.

4 Review the performance of the portfolio as a whole, as well as each asset class and each individual investment.

5 Prepare your annual tax return.

Managing your asset allocation

Of these tasks, the most important is reviewing and maintaining the asset allocation. It's this allocation that will primarily determine your portfolio's return and risk.

Over time, your portfolio will move out of alignment with what you originally set as your desired asset allocation. This is because some of your investments, especially shares, will change in value.

Say, for example, you start with $100,000, and want 50% ($50,000) invested in shares and 50% in other asset classes. After six months, you notice that the value of your shares has increased to $60,000 and your total portfolio is now worth $110,000. This means your shares are now around 55% of the portfolio and the other asset classes are only 45%.

To optimise the return on your portfolio, you should bring the asset allocation back in line with what you originally set by selling part of your share portfolio so the shares are valued at $55,000 (50% of $110,000). The money you make should be reinvested in the other asset classes to bring them back to 50%.

Similarly, if your shares were to fall in value to $40,000 after six months, they would drop to 44% of the total portfolio ($90,000 divided by $40,000). You should rebalance by purchasing more shares, funded by reducing the value of other investments in the portfolio. You should then hold shares to the value of $45,000, or 50% of $90,000.

Why is it necessary to do this?

When you analyse the effect of your actions, the answer is obvious. You will be selling off shares when prices are high, and buying more shares when prices are low. In this way, you will optimise the return on your portfolio.

Uneducated investors will tend to do the exact opposite. Typically, they will base investment decisions on past performance, on the assumption that such trends will continue indefinitely. Seeing a rapid and sustained rise in share prices, for example, they will buy shares in the expectation of a continued upward trend.

An astute investor, on the other hand, will realise that a sustained rapid rise in shares prices is always followed by a fall. Lo and behold, when the uneducated investor sees share prices fall they panic and sell. The end result? The investor has bought shares when prices are high and sold them when they are low, a good way to lose money.

Employing a portfolio manager

You can manage your own investment portfolio or have it managed for you by a financial adviser. You should consider managing your own portfolio if:

- You have a small portfolio – say, under $50,000.
- Your portfolio consists mostly of investments, such as fixed-interest investments, that do not require a lot of monitoring.
- You have an interest in investments, and an affinity with numbers.
- You have spare time on your hands to research and monitor your portfolio.

Evaluating the performance of your investment portfolio

If you are an investor, rather than a speculator, your target will be to optimise your return over a long time frame – say, five to ten years. As an investor, your choice is between a stable portfolio that produces a consistent but low return and a more volatile portfolio that produces a variable return in the short term but a high return over the long term.

Hoarders and **achievers** will look for stability.

Entrepreneurs and **thrill-seekers** will be comfortable with volatility in order to get a higher return.

Stability v. volatility

The portfolio most likely to consistently produce a positive return is one made up entirely of fixed-interest investments, unless of course there is a default of capital or interest.

If your portfolio includes growth assets such as shares, its value will move up and down. Some years it will perform well; other years it will produce a negative return. Don't make the mistake of comparing its performance year-by-year with a fixed interest portfolio: this is akin to comparing apples and oranges. There will always be years when a fixed interest portfolio would have done better. Knowing that in advance can save you a lot of anguish, and should convince you that commentators who compare the annual performance of growth portfolios with fixed interest portfolios are simply scaremongers.

In the short term, compare the performance of each asset class in your portfolio against the market index that is relevant to that asset class. Your aim should be to do better than the market. If your share portfolio decreased in value by 15% but the market index went down by 30%, you did well with your shares.

In the long term, your aim should be to produce a better return (after tax and fees) than you would have achieved by leaving your money in the bank for the same period. How much better depends on the degree of risk you are willing to take.

Your investment time frame and why you must invest in shares – especially if you are retired

Simply put, your investment time frame is the period at the end of which you plan to use up your capital. For example, if you are investing for retirement, or to work less, your time frame is *not* the period until your retirement: it is the period until you will need to *spend* your capital, rather than using it to produce income.

If you are aged 50 and plan to retire or work less at 65, your investment time frame is not 15 years but 25 or more, depending how long you live and how fast you use up your capital when you're retired. If you have recently retired, even if you plan to have nothing left for your children it will still take you some time to use up all your investment capital; at least part of your portfolio can be invested for ten years or more.

Investing over a long time frame means some of your investments should be in assets that grow in value. Say, for example, you invest $100,000 when you retire and choose to live off the income produced by your investment capital. Assuming a gross return of 6% on your money, or 4.8% after tax, you will generate an after-tax return of $4,800 a year to supplement your pension.

Sound good? Well, it might be fine for the first few years, but after ten years of inflation at 3%, your capital will be worth only about $73,700 in today's dollars, and your income will be only the equivalent of $3,540 a year. That's a drop of around 26% in your capital and your income. To maintain your income, you will need to start using up some of your capital, which in turn will reduce your investment income even further.

As an example, according to government statistics, if you went shopping in 1987 and filled your basket up with food to the value of $100, that same basket of food would cost $130 in 1997 and $167 in 2007. If you retired at age 65 today, at the same rate of increase, that basket of food would cost around $279 in twenty years' time.

The only kind of investment (excluding leveraged investments) that will produce an after-tax return great enough to keep ahead of inflation in the long term, while still producing an income, is shares.

Over a ten-year period, you could reasonably expect to get a return of 8% after tax on a diversified share portfolio of $100,000. Your net income would average around $8,000 a year. This would enable you to retain income of $4,800 and grow your portfolio by $3,200 a year. This way it would be growing by an average of 3.2% a year, enough to keep ahead of inflation – thus preserving your capital and income in today's dollars.

Of course, just as it doesn't make sense to have all your money tied up in fixed interest where it can get eaten away by tax and inflation, nor does it make sense to have it all in shares, which are volatile. As always, the best course of action is to spread your money across the asset classes in accordance with your preferred asset allocation.

Investor or speculator?

Speculators seek to make short-term gains on their investment portfolio, usually through taking a high level of risk in anticipation of a high return. This is very different from investors, who seek to make a good return over the long term.

Speculators may buy and sell shares on a daily basis to take advantage of price fluctuations and mispricing in the market. They may anticipate market trends to their advantage. For example, foreseeing a property upturn in a particular geographic area, they will buy and sell to make a short-term capital gain.

Speculators keep a close eye on short-term price changes in their investment assets, whereas investors don't. An investor is aware that the only prices that matter for an investment asset are the purchase price and the sale price: anything in between is irrelevant. If you are intending to sell an asset in ten years time, you don't need to worry about what its price is today, or what it is expected to be next year.

Both investors and speculators know that markets move in cycles. A speculator will attempt to buy at the lowest possible point and sell at the highest possible point, all within a short time frame. Because the time frame is short, the speculator must accurately guess the market peaks and troughs.

An investor is less concerned with picking these peaks and troughs. His or her strategy is to hold an asset long enough that, even if it were purchased close to the peak of the market, it will have been through enough market cycles with an upward trend that it can still be sold for a good return.

One of the biggest mistakes you can make when creating wealth is to take on too much risk too soon. Starting off a portfolio with speculative investments is a good way to get nowhere fast. Entrepreneurs need to be particularly careful about this.

If you have no experience of investing, you may make mistakes. Practise being an investor first by saving regularly into a diversified portfolio or fund until you have built up a solid base of $50,000–$100,000. With this amount of capital and investment experience behind you, you can look around for some speculative opportunities.

> Entrepreneurs and thrill-seekers are attracted to speculation. Hoarders and achievers are more comfortable as investors.

Tax and speculation

If you are a speculator, you need to carefully consider your tax position. If you are deemed to be a trader, or it is clear that you are purchasing and selling assets for the purpose of making capital gain as a form of income, you may be liable for tax on the capital gains you make.

Home equity release

Getting to retirement age without having created a nest egg? You are not alone – a large percentage of the population is in the same boat.

You may be a thrill-seeker who spends your life living for the moment, or an achiever who has accumulated lifestyle assets but no assets capable of producing an investment return. On the other hand, you may simply have had bad luck – lost your job, lost money in a business venture, suffered serious long-term illness, or lost a partner through death or separation.

If you are lucky enough to own your own home, you will have a valuable asset. However, you will not be able to access the wealth tied up in your house unless you sell it, or take out a mortgage on it. For most retired people, the prospect of having a mortgage is daunting as a pension may provide enough to live on but not enough to repay debt.

For some people, the answer can be home equity release.

Home equity release is a kind of mortgage that enables you to remain living in your house while being able to access the wealth that is tied up in it.

You will not have to repay either the principal or the interest in your lifetime. Instead, the interest will compound, and both principal and compounded interest will be repaid when the house is finally sold.

The amount of money you can borrow is determined by a percentage of the house's value based on the age of the youngest occupier, and set at a level that aims to retain around 50% to 60% of the value of the house for when it is sold.

The interest rate on a home equity loan is higher than the interest on a standard mortgage.

In taking out a home equity loan, you are essentially using up part of your children's inheritance, but these days it is becoming less common for children to either expect or need an inheritance, and less common for parents to feel obliged to leave one.

As an alternative, you can ask the beneficiaries of your estate – usually your children – to lend you the money you need so as to preserve their entitlement. This way the interest costs will be less, but your beneficiaries will have to either borrow the money themselves and make the necessary repayments, or forgo interest on money they would otherwise have invested elsewhere.

Doing it this way can get messy when there are several beneficiaries, especially when they may not all be in a position to provide the necessary funds. If some, but not all, are in a position to help, an agreement will need to be reached among the beneficiaries as to how the estate is to be divided so those who have provided funds will not be not disadvantaged.

I have helped many clients arrange a home equity loan, and the difference it has made to their lives has been incredible. One couple in their eighties had emigrated from Britain many years earlier and had never been able to afford a return visit. As a result of the loan, they were able to go back and meet some of their grandchildren for the first time, and catch up with other relatives they hadn't seen since they emigrated.

You can also use a home equity loan to upgrade the standard of house you are living in. Another couple I helped used a home equity loan to buy the retirement home of their dreams by topping up the difference between the value of their previous home and their new, maintenance-free home. The difference this made to their happiness was heart-warming to see.

Wealth-creation strategies

We have looked at a number of different ways of creating wealth. Now let's put it all together.

For most investors, your schedule will be:

1. As soon as you have sufficient surplus income, join a superannuation scheme that is subsidised by the government and/or your employer – for example, KiwiSaver.
2. Pay off short-term debt, such as credit-card and hire purchase debt.
3. Build up an emergency fund.
4. Purchase your first house, and live in it yourself and/or rent to others.
5. Pay off long-term debt, such as your mortgage (unless the interest on the debt is tax-deductible against investment income).
6. Invest for medium- and long-term goals using your own funds and, where appropriate, borrowed funds.

Different money personalities will be at different stages of this list, and will find some items easier to do than others.

HOARDER

As a hoarder you value safety and security above all else. You were probably the first in the queue to join a subsidised superannuation scheme. Your debt will be under control and you are probably trying to pay it off over the shortest possible period. You are very likely to have an emergency fund.

Your biggest challenge is investing for your medium-term and long-term goals. Because you are so security-conscious, you will accept a lower return to achieve peace of mind. Over the long term, the return on your savings and investments will struggle to keep ahead of inflation and tax. You will say no to investment opportunities that could make you a lot of money because you will be afraid to take the risk. You will create a good amount of wealth in your lifetime, but it could be even more if you loosened up a little.

- Take a few risks. Set aside a percentage of your wealth, even if only 20%, to invest in opportunities that are risky, but have potential for high returns.
- Minimise your risk through diversification, research, and involving experts whom you trust.
- Don't take on high-risk investing that is well beyond your tolerance level: one failure and you are bound to retreat to your safe haven of low-risk investing. Unlike an entrepreneur, you will see failure as a disaster, rather than as an opportunity to learn.
- Increase your expectations. You *can* create more wealth than you think, and you *can* do the things you dream of. Set your sights high: not only can you create more wealth, but you deserve it. Make a conscious effort not to be held back by feelings of guilt, or the fear that you may lose everything you have.

ACHIEVER

As an achiever, you have probably joined a subsidised superannuation scheme. However, you are living from pay-day to pay-day because you have taken on as much debt as you can afford. You spend before you save, rather than saving before you spend. If you have followed the advice in the previous section and found ways to cut back on your spending and/or increase your income, your focus needs to be first on building up an emergency fund, and secondly on paying off your debt as quickly as possible.

- Get into the habit of saving before you spend, rather than spending money you don't have.
- Decide what's really important to you in life, and set some clear goals in that area.
- Set the contributions into your subsidised superannuation scheme at the minimum required to attract the maximum subsidy.
- Build up an emergency fund.
- Work out how much you need to set aside each week from now until the age at which you want to be able to choose not to work, or to

substantially cut down your workload, in order to pay off your mortgage *and* provide for your retirement goals. If you feel you can keep your debt under control, put all that amount into repaying your mortgage, so that it is paid off well before you stop work, and then put the equivalent amount into a fund for your retirement. However, a safer strategy is to do a bit of both.

- Diversify your investing to reduce the amount of risk.
- Consider using the equity in your home to purchase investment properties or to set up your own business. In other words, become more of an entrepreneur.

ENTREPRENEUR

As an entrepreneur, you thrive on uncertainty. You want to do better than the average person and achieve as much out of life as you can. You'll invest any resources you can lay your hands on – other people's as well as your own. You believe that you can make good financial decisions, and will be wary of advice from others unless they can demonstrate proven skills and experience. You expect to have failures along the way to success, and see these as learning experiences. You also believe that if you lose money you can make it again.

- Take educated risks: do research rather than relying on your gut instinct.
- Put together a team of highly skilled experts whose knowledge and experience can help you achieve your ambitious goals. Make sure you pick people who are the best in their field and have a proven track record.
- Don't gamble with everything you have. As you make money, set some aside in a safe fund to create a store of wealth that is invested with a low level of risk. This way your longer term goals will not be in jeopardy.
- Borrow to invest, but put limits on your borrowing. Make sure your leverage portfolio can withstand a change in the economic environment, such as increased interest rates or reduced returns.

- Don't set impossible targets that require you to take huge risks. Be realistic with what you can achieve, and objective, rather than emotional, with your decisions.

THRILL-SEEKER

Of all the money personality types, you will be in the weakest position to create wealth. You will be starting from a low base (if anything at all) and you'll have a large amount of debt. You probably won't be able to afford to join a subsidised superannuation scheme because you can barely keep up with your present commitments.

At the extreme, you may even be in the situation where your income is insufficient for you to repay your debt commitments, and you are going deeper into debt just to survive. Wealth-creation strategies will be of no use unless you have stopped adding to your debt and created some excess income that you can use to pay it off. If you're not at this stage, read the previous section again!

- Take small steps. Start with one short-term, achievable goal. Once you've achieved that, set another short-term goal.
- Your first goal is to clear your short-term debt. Decide on a set amount you will apply each pay-day. Focus on one debt at a time, starting with the debt with the highest interest rate.
- Get into the habit of saving before you spend, rather than spending money you don't have.
- Decide what's really important to you in life, and set some clear goals in that area.
- Build up an emergency fund.
- As soon as you can afford it, join a subsidised superannuation scheme.
- Set a goal to purchase a house that you will live in and/or rent to others. If you have left it too late to be able to pay off the mortgage by the time you wish to retire or work less, consider converting the remainder to a home equity mortgage once you are eligible.

Protect your nest egg

Even if you have a good track record of regularly putting money aside, you can find yourself in dire straits if you have not protected your savings.

Once you have built up your wealth it is vital to protect it. Most of us will suffer several adverse experiences in our lives, whether the loss of a job, a major illness or a relationship breakdown. These unexpected events can trip us up financially. If you have a large amount of debt, the consequences may be tragic. If you have savings, they may destroy some or all of them.

Risk protection is an often overlooked aspect of wealth creation, but if you create wealth and don't protect it you may lose it. The shortest recorded period of time lies between the minute you put money away for a rainy day and the unexpected arrival of rain.

> Thrill-seekers and entrepreneurs often overlook risk protection so gamble unnecessarily.

Key ways to protect your savings:

- Set up an emergency fund, or access to credit, that can cover your living expenses for three to six months.
- Review your insurance needs, particularly if the strategies in your wealth-creation plan have increased your level of financial risk.
- Plan your estate with wills, family trusts, and enduring powers of attorney to preserve your wealth for your children and grandchildren.
- As a large percentage of relationships do not survive, make sure your wealth-creation strategies take into account the implications of the Property (Relationships) Act. This is particularly so if you are in, or may enter, a second relationship.

Emergency fund

A first step is to create an emergency fund, or arrange access to credit, that can help pay living expenses for you and your family until you are back on track. As a rule of thumb, you should have access to enough funds to keep you going for three to six months. For more information on how to do this, refer to pages 94–95.

Insurance

To put in place the rest of your risk-protection strategy, ask yourself what risks you may face. Things that often erode wealth are:

- the premature death of a family member
- loss of income through illness or disability.

Now try to put a dollar value on the amount involved. The best way is to ask:

> How much money would be needed for me and/or my family in the event of:
> – my premature death?
> – a traumatic illness in the family?
> – an illness or disability that left me unable to work for a long time?

For example, if you were to die prematurely, you might want your partner to have a mortgage-free home, no personal debt, and a regular weekly income until such time as all your children were at school. How much would this cost?

Having put a dollar figure on each risk, consider taking out insurance. Obviously insurance has a cost, so while your ideal solution may be to insure away all risk, premiums for this will probably be too high to be affordable.

> You should identify the most important areas to cover within a limited insurance budget.

You may also choose to 'self-insure' – that is, to take on all or part of a particular risk yourself. One example of partial self-insurance would be taking out medical insurance to cover the costs of surgery, but not to cover the cost of visits to your family doctor.

Similarly, income-protection insurance premiums can be lowered by increasing the 'stand-down' period – that is, the time you must wait until the benefit is payable. As a general rule, it is better to reduce premiums in this way, rather than by reducing the cover or other benefits.

Exclusions and loadings

One of the biggest issues you will face when applying for insurance is to obtain cover that does not exclude existing medical conditions, or load on your premium if you are considered a high risk – because you are overweight, for instance, or have a family history of illness.

Don't leave it until it is too late. The older you are when you apply, the more likely it is that you will have an exclusion or a loading.

If you do find yourself in this situation, try a number of different insurance companies. Policies vary, and some insurance underwriters are more lenient than others.

Review your insurance regularly

I recommend to my clients that they review their insurance needs at least once a year. You should also review them if your circumstances change – for example, if you increase your level of debt, enter a new relationship, have more children or set up a new business.

More information on specific types of insurance is set out on pages 262–66.

The 'it'll never happen to me' myth

One of the worst mistakes you can make when looking at your insurance is to think that nothing bad will ever happen to you. Never, ever, make that mistake.

A colleague of mine arranged a mortgage for a young couple in their thirties who had two small children and were buying their first house. She repeatedly advised the couple to take out life insurance at the same time, but they repeatedly refused. Within a few weeks, the husband died suddenly of a brain aneurysm, leaving his wife struggling to pay the mortgage while living on a benefit. Imagine how different life would have been for the wife and children if there had been insurance to pay off the mortgage, and provide a lump sum that could be invested to produce extra income or used to pay child-care costs.

In another case, a colleague tried to persuade a client in his forties to take out some life insurance, but to no avail. Believe it or not, that very same day the client was killed by a car while walking across a road. No doubt every insurance broker has similar stories to tell.

On the other side of the ledger are the good stories. One of my large investment clients is the widow of an executive who was killed in a freak accident, but left his family well provided for because of his good insurance cover.

Another client who discovered she had breast cancer was able to use a lump-sum payment from her trauma cover to pay for specialist treatment, and to go on a well-deserved holiday once the treatment was over. As she also had income-protection insurance, she could return to work gradually as her energy levels increased.

If your income were to cease for a while, would you be able to maintain your lifestyle and meet your financial commitments?

Major health conditions such as cancer, heart attacks and strokes can strike anyone. How would waiting for major surgery affect you or your family? Would your partner or family have to take care of you? If you died, would they be able to maintain their lifestyle?

Did you know?

- One in seven people die during their working lives.
- Women are more likely to get, but survive, a serious illness.
- From age 45, illness is the major cause of death. For men, heart disease is the most common, and for women cancer.
- One in three people will suffer a major illness or injury that will stop them working for three months or longer.
- One in two men and one in four women will suffer a major illness or injury before they reach 65.
- Of every ten men and ten women currently aged 25, five men and seven women will, before they turn 65, suffer an illness or accident that will prevent them working for at least a month. Of these, at least a third will still be unable to work 12 months later.
- 29 percent of New Zealanders have a diagnosed long-term illness or disability.

Estate planning

I am always amazed at the number of people I come across who don't have a will, or any form of estate planning. This includes even well-educated professionals, and people with hundreds of thousands of dollars in assets.

Wills

If you own assets you need a will. If you die intestate – that is, without a will – it may cost your family a lot of money to sort out your affairs, they will endure delays getting access to your estate, and it may not be settled in the way you would have wished.

You can draw up a will yourself: there are free templates available online. However, it is usually better to have a will drawn up by an expert such as a lawyer or trustee company, as there are many complicating factors, particularly if you have had more than one life partner.

In the absence of a will, your estate will be dealt with by the Court. Here's what will happen in New Zealand.

If you have a spouse or partner, but no children or parents:
your whole estate will go to your spouse or partner.

If you have a spouse or partner, and children:
your spouse or partner will receive all personal chattels, the first $121,500, and one-third of the remainder;
your children will receive two-thirds of the remainder.

If you have children, but no current spouse or partner:
the whole estate will pass in equal shares to your children.

If you have parents, but no spouse, partner or children:
the whole estate will pass equally to your parents.

If you have a spouse or partner and parents, but no children:
your spouse or partner will receive all personal chattels, the first $121,500 and two-thirds of the remainder;
your parents will receive one-third of the remainder.

If you have no spouse, partner, children or parents:
your whole estate will pass to certain blood relatives.

De facto couples – the three-year rule

When it comes to dividing up property, in New Zealand de facto couples, including same-sex, who have been together for three years or more have the same rights as married couples. However, if you and your partner have been together less than three years and you die without a will, your partner may get nothing from your estate.

Testamentary trusts

In your will it is possible to set up a testamentary trust. This is a trust that will be formed after your death to look after your assets on behalf of your beneficiaries, and in accordance with your wishes. This can be a useful way of protecting assets if your beneficiaries are not trustworthy, or you want to make sure your assets are not gobbled up by fees if your spouse has to go into care.

In the latter case, you and your partner can divide your assets in half, with each surviving spouse being left as a beneficiary of the estate, with a right to any income from it but not the capital. That way, the capital is not the property of the surviving spouse, and is preserved for the next generation.

Family trusts

Trusts are an increasingly common way of protecting and managing assets. Putting your assets into a trust can protect them from creditors and relationship property claims because technically they are no longer your assets. There are also tax benefits. See 'Reducing your tax', page 130.

You can create a trust deed, setting out how the trust will operate, with the help of a solicitor. You, as settlor, then transfer your assets to the trustees of the trust, who manage them in accordance with the trust deed.

One of the roles of trustees is to make payments from the trust to its beneficiaries. You, the settlor, can be a trustee *and* a beneficiary. However, it is usual for there to be another trustee who is independent – that is, neither a settlor nor a beneficiary of the trust.

Enduring powers of attorney

An enduring power of attorney is a legal document by which you appoint a person or a trust company to act on your behalf when you are no longer able to manage your affairs for some reason. Many people think their family can just take over, but this isn't true. Instead, the Family Court may be appointed to take on the role and this will cost time and money.

An enduring power of attorney can be used only while you are alive. You may be ill, or have had an accident, or be no longer mentally capable of managing your affairs. Or you may be overseas, and want to leave a person or trust company in New Zealand to make decisions about your property and investments in your absence.

An enduring power of attorney is very flexible: you can give or retain as much control as you like. You can:

- specify if the power of attorney is to begin immediately, or at some time in the future.
- allow the attorney to look after all or just some of your assets.
- cancel or change the power of attorney at any time, provided you have the mental capacity to do so.
- appoint two or more people, or a trust company, to be your attorney if the document relates to your property or other assets.

Everyone should have a power of attorney. By setting one up you can be confident that, should you need assistance in the future, your assets and personal welfare will be properly managed by people whom you trust.

There are two types of enduring power of attorney, one for your property and one for your personal care and welfare. The first allows another person or a trust company to look after your affairs, such as running a business, filing tax returns, supervising investments, maintaining your home and collecting rents, and, should you die, your funeral.

The second permits another person to make personal decisions such as accommodation arrangements, purchase of clothing and personal items, and medical decisions for you. It can become effective only if and when you are mentally incapable of making those decisions yourself.

The main difference between an ordinary power of attorney and an enduring one is that an ordinary attorney's powers lapse if the donor (the person granting the power) becomes incompetent to look after his or her affairs, while enduring powers commence at that point. However, the fact that the donor is incompetent means there are potential problems. For instance, if you name your spouse as your attorney, his or her powers do not lapse if you separate. In that situation, your ex-spouse may be the last person you want as your attorney.

Similarly, there is potential for you, if you are incompetent, to be taken advantage of or bullied by your attorney. When money is involved, your attorney may be tempted to put their own interests ahead of yours, especially when your state of mind is such that you wouldn't know the difference, so choose your attorney carefully. You should appoint only someone whom you trust implicitly. This may be a friend, a relative or a trustee company.

Finally, because an enduring power of attorney is a legal document, you should get legal advice before signing.

Property (Relationships) Act planning

In New Zealand, the Property (Relationships) Act applies automatically to all married couples, and to those who have been living together in a de facto situation for a minimum of three years, whether they are of the same or opposite sex. It applies whether a relationship ends through separation or death, and can override the provisions of a deceased partner's will.

The definition of a de facto relationship is not black and white. It is decided by the Court on a number of different factors, which may include:

- the length of the relationship
- the extent to which you shared a home
- the degree to which your finances were merged
- how your property was owned and used
- whether you had a sexual relationship
- how you cared for and supported any children of either of you
- who performed household duties
- your mutual commitment to a shared life:
  - whether others saw you as a couple; and
  - any other appropriate matters.

Two people can live together, for example as flatmates, without their relationship being considered de facto. On the other hand, a couple can live in separate residences and still be considered de facto because their finances are linked, they have children together, and others regard them as a couple.

Under the Act, the assets of married couples, and couples in a de facto relationship for three years or more, are shared equally if the relationship ends through separation or death. The only way to change this is for the couple to enter into a contracting-out agreement, which states how they wish to divide their assets when the relationship ends. Assets held in a family trust created before the start of relationship are usually considered to be separate, rather than relationship, property, so trusts can also be used to protect personal assets and to alter the normal 50:50 split.

Where separate property, such as a gift, trust money or an inheritance, becomes intermingled with other relationship property, it may be classified as relationship property. Unless you are absolutely certain your relationship will survive, you should therefore make sure that any separate property, especially gifts and inheritances, are kept absolutely separate from your other property, and that there is a clear trail that shows where that property has come from.

> If you are in doubt about relationship property, always seek legal advice.

Protection strategies

Risk-takers, such as entrepreneurs and thrill-seekers, are in particular need of strategies to minimise their exposure to risk and protect their wealth. Hoarders and achievers, who are naturally more risk-averse, also need protection strategies but for a different reason: to give them the confidence to engage in methods of wealth-creation that would otherwise be outside their comfort zone.

Wealth-protection tips

HOARDERS

You are afraid of loss, and so have no doubt organised good insurance cover. Watch out for over-insuring, especially as your wealth grows, your debt disappears and your children leave home.

You will have an up to date will, but have you looked at whether you need a family trust to protect your wealth in the long term and for the sake of the next generation?

As a hoarder, you are likely to leave a significant sum behind, so make sure it is safe. Here are my tips.

- Don't be afraid to reduce or cancel your insurance cover once it is no longer required.
- Consider whether a family trust would be of benefit to protect your wealth for the next generation.
- Don't forget to grant enduring powers of attorney.

ACHIEVERS

You are motivated by success and are always looking for ways to increase your income. For that reason you probably earn as much as, if not more than, your peers.

The trouble is that, while your income grows, so do your outgoings. As you are living from pay day to pay day, you will be in difficulty if you are suddenly in a situation where no income is coming in. Think about what would happen if you were no longer able to work for an extended period of time.

My tips:

- Review your need for income-protection insurance and trauma cover.
- Have an emergency fund on hand that will help you through the first few months of being off work if you suffer a serious illness, and will cover any unexpected bills.
- Make sure you have updated your will or granted enduring powers of attorney.

- If you have considerable wealth tied up in your house, consider whether it should be owned by a family trust.

ENTREPRENEUR

You are so busy making money you may have overlooked a few details, such as keeping your will up to date and preparing enduring powers of attorney. You are a risk taker, but there are ways you can significantly reduce your exposure to risk which won't interfere in your grand plans. My tips are:

- Use legal structures such as limited liability companies and trusts to protect your personal assets from creditors or from business failure.
- You are a key person in your business and in your family, so use life insurance to protect your business ventures and your family from suffering in the event of your demise.
- Make sure you have updated your will.

THRILL-SEEKER

When you're struggling to keep on top of debt and spending more than you should, there's often no money left to pay insurance premiums. As a risk-taker, you're prepared to gamble that you won't need to make an insurance claim and can therefore do without life insurance. That's less of an issue while age is on your side, but if you wait until you are older to buy insurance cover you may find that you have developed health problems that will make your premiums more expensive, or certain health risks may be excluded from your cover. My tips are:

- Put in place some basic insurance cover that you can add to once your financial situation improves.
- Have an emergency fund that will help you through the first few months of being off work if you suffer a serious illness, and to cover any unexpected bills.
- If you haven't prepared a will yet, do it now. No excuses! Organise your enduring powers of attorney at the same time.

STEP 5

Record your wealth-creation plan

CONGRATULATIONS! LOOK HOW FAR YOU'VE COME. If you have followed the steps in this book, you have worked out the role of money in your life and set some goals. You have developed strategies to save money and set up a system to create wealth automatically. You have settled on an investment strategy for your savings, and taken steps to protect your wealth.

Now you need to write down your goals and strategies in a wealth-creation plan that can be shared with others – such as your family, your business partners and your trusted advisers. That way you can make sure it happens.

Your plan and your money personality

HOARDER

Your plan will be conservative in nature and won't involve much change, so you may think recording it will be easy. Your first challenge, though, is to think outside the square and be more ambitious in your goals. Don't settle for the same-old same-old. (Your second challenge will be actually carrying out your plan. Hoarders sometimes lack the confidence to do this, and will think of any number of excuses as to why the plan can't be implemented.)

ACHIEVER

Achievers are usually the best planners. You are goal-oriented, and will have a clear plan for how to get to where you want to be. However, that plan is probably in your head. Put it on a piece of paper where it can be shared with others – and then make a supreme effort to stick to it.

ENTREPRENEUR

You will have a clear vision of where you want to go, but may lack details as to how you are going to get there. It is likely that you will have so many ideas you will lack the focus to achieve any of them. You need to break your grand vision down into small, intermediate goals that you can achieve one after the other. Without this detailed step-by-step approach you will be readily distracted, and could find yourself leaping from one grand vision to the next.

THRILL-SEEKER

Being led more by impulse than rationality, you find it difficult to make plans and stick to them. Your best approach is to enlist a hoarder or an achiever – whether a partner, friend or professional adviser – to help you formulate, write down and implement your plan.

How to write your plan

By writing down your plan you will clarify your thinking, have a benchmark against which to check your progress, and be able to share your vision with others who can offer support and encouragement.

Here are the essentials.

1 Set measurable targets and objectives *with time-lines.*

2 Identify and note the support you will need to achieve each step.

I suggest you start with these headings:

- Guiding principles
- Goals
- Limiting factors
- Opportunities
- Strategies and objectives for:
  - cutting your costs without sacrificing your lifestyle
  - increasing your net income with little or no extra effort
  - using technology to create wealth automatically
  - multiplying your money
  - protecting your nest egg
- Support needed
- Immediate action – things to do today.

Goals and strategies that are written down are many times more likely to be achieved than goals and strategies that are not.

Guiding principles

Your plan should start by defining your guiding principles, as discussed on page 92. Examples of guiding principles are:

- security
- happiness
- peace of mind
- fun and adventure
- supporting family and friends
- making a difference to other people's lives

Goals

On pages 94–97 we looked at three types of goal:

- Compulsory goal – emergency funds
- Working-life goals
- Retirement goals

For each of these you need to specify a time frame, and the amount of money needed to achieve the goal.

Start and finish lines

The biggest enemy of wealth creation is procrastination – putting things off. This is a particular threat for hoarders and achievers, who are less impulsive than entrepreneurs and thrill-seekers.

To avoid procrastination, be specific about when the steps in your plan will start and finish. Times can be adjusted along the way if they turn out to be unrealistic, but they should exist. Without deadlines it's easy to lose motivation and momentum.

Limiting factors

Inevitably, there will be hazards and handicaps to deal with along the way. You may be made redundant. You may have health problems. You may find you lack knowledge in some areas. Do not give up!

Take steps to minimise the effect of these setbacks. It will be easier to do this if you have worked out strategies in advance. If you are self-employed, for example, a limiting factor may be the uncertainty of your income, which may fluctuate from month to month, and year to year. Counteract this problem by creating a cash buffer.

You can even turn setbacks into positives. For example, if you are faced with redundancy, you can come up with ways of creating alternative income streams, or retrain to open up new employment opportunities.

Opportunities

Opportunities may arise that make it easier for you to achieve your goals. You may have a relative or friend who knows a lot about property investment, and can advise you about suitable properties. There may be a spare room in your house that you can rent out, or a piece of unused land on your property that can be subdivided. A friend may suggest a new business venture.

Do some brainstorming – and remember to keep an open mind. If you are a risk-averse hoarder or achiever, you will think of a dozen reasons why a promising idea won't work. Your thinking may have become blinkered. You may be putting constraints and limitations on what you can do that don't really exist.

Talk over opportunities with someone who knows your circumstances: they may see opportunities for you that you can't see.

Strategies

You have determined your goals – what you want to achieve. Now you need to plan *how* to achieve them.

You will need strategies to cover each of the remaining five wealth-creation steps. There will be a number of different ways to achieve your goals: choose those that best fit your guiding principles, opportunities and limitations.

Next to each of your strategies, note something that you will do in the next 24 hours to start the ball rolling. It may be a simple thing, such as calling into your bank to rearrange your bank accounts, making an appointment to see a financial adviser, or pulling out your insurance policies to see how much cover you have.

Objectives

Well-written objectives turn dreams into reality by focussing your mind on each milestone you need to attain. They convert strategies into small achievable tasks that don't seem so daunting. Once recorded, they become the benchmarks by which you judge your progress.

To be effective, your objectives should be:

- specific, measurable and achievable
- time-bound
- acted upon
- visible every day
- consistent with your guiding principles
- reviewed regularly – at least every 12 months.

Get a support team!

Your chances of success will be greatly enhanced if you call upon experts and other resources. You may need assistance from an accountant or lawyer to help you set up and run a company. You may need a business mentor. You may benefit by joining an association such as your local chamber of commerce, or property investors' association.

It's also useful to have a general support person, who can act a sounding-board for ideas and help resolve problems and difficulties. Choose this person carefully.

STEP 6

Make it happen

YOU NOW HAVE A PLAN. IT'S TIME TO GET MOVING.

The biggest hurdle is taking the first step. This is no different to writing the first paragraph of a book or turning the first sod on a building project: taking that one step gives you the feeling you are on your way, and encourages you to believe in yourself and keep going.

It's not necessary for this first step to be big. On the contrary, the smaller the step the easier it will be to take and the more likely you will be to act. Start with small steps and you will be rewarded with success and the motivation to take on bigger, more important tasks.

Many people are great at coming up with ideas, but never put them into action. Others are better at doing than planning, but without a plan their efforts flounder and fail.

Success = plan + action

Try and do something every day to move you closer to your goals. Remember, if you do what you have always done, you will get what you have always got.

How to improve your chance of success

Putting your plan into action is much harder than writing it, but there are a number of things you can do to make it easier and head to success. The biggest mistakes are, first, thinking you can do everything yourself and, second, trying to do too much too soon. Here are some simple ways of overcoming these problems.

Share your plan with someone

It may be a partner, good friend, family member or adviser. The more you talk about your plan, the more committed you will be to it, and the more it will stay top-of-mind. Ask the person to quiz you regularly about progress. This will keep you motivated.

He or she can also remind you about your goals when they see you doing something inconsistent with your plan. If you are a thrill-seeker and want to become less impulsive, ask your friends to remind you of this when they see you acting impulsively.

Get expert assistance in areas where you lack confidence

No matter how clever you think you are, there is always more you can learn. Even though you will probably have to pay for this advice, it will minimise your risk of making costly mistakes. You will learn how to manage your affairs better and take control of your money. Getting expert assistance is a good way for hoarders and achievers to gain the confidence to try new ways of creating wealth.

Keep focusing on the benefits

To change behaviour you have to be highly motivated. If you find your motivation dropping, remind yourself of the benefits you'll gain, and try and stay focused on them. Staying focused is particularly important for hoarders and thrill-seekers, who are inclined to lack the motivation to create wealth.

Don't set a lot of difficult things to do at once

It's better to start with a few small steps that will make a big difference, and get these bedded in. Setting up your bank accounts and systemising your money management is a good place to start. Once you have the basic structure in place, you can make further refinements until you come up with the system that works best for you.

If you are an entrepreneur with a million ideas for creating wealth, a plan will help you prioritise your ideas so you can focus on one or two key areas.

Regularly measure how well you are doing

- Check your bank accounts several times a week. (You can easily do this online.)
- Monitor your investments quarterly.
- Calculate your net worth at least once a year.

If things are going well, reward yourself

Allow yourself to do something financially irresponsible (as long as it's not *too* irresponsible). Share your success with other people. Celebrating success is a particularly useful motivational technique for thrill-seekers who are aiming to reduce debt.

Setbacks

Of course, things may not work out as you intend. Maybe you and your partner can't agree on priorities and strategies. Maybe you do agree, but one of you doesn't follow the plan. That's probably a sign that communication between you isn't as good as it should be, or that your hasn't *really* bought into the plan. Either way, it's time to go back to the drawing board until you've come up with a plan to which both of you are committed, and a process for making sure you both stay on track.

Sometimes a plan may fail though factors outside your control. Perhaps you've tried something with an element of risk, and luck hasn't gone your way. Perhaps the economy has taken a nosedive, or mortgage interest rates have soared.

This reinforces the need to keep an eye on what's happening around you so you don't get caught out. Stay informed. Read the business pages in the newspaper. Regularly visit websites that can keep you up to date with market trends.

While it is important to have a good plan, it should never be set in concrete. Your circumstances may change, whether a change in a relationship, a new family member, illness, death, change of employment, or changes in your personal values and attitudes.

Your plan should be reviewed at least once a year, and whenever your circumstances or your goals change.

> If something hasn't worked out according to plan, whatever you do don't panic.

Try to understand *why* it hasn't worked out and make a logical, rational decision on how to remedy the situation. Sometimes your best strategy is just to wait and see what happens next.

Dealing with sudden change

Sometimes change can come more quickly than you might expect, and be traumatic in its effect.

Death of a partner

Death of a partner ranks as one of the most traumatic life changes. It can take a year or more for the emotional impact to fade sufficiently for you to be able to make rational decisions.

Keep to three basic rules.

1. Don't make any significant financial or lifestyle decisions until you feel on an even keel emotionally. This way, you will avoid making decisions you later regret.
2. Keep your options open. Don't make any financial or other commitments until you are certain of your future plans.
3. Make your own decisions. During a time of traumatic change, numerous people will offer you advice. Listen to what they say, but be selective as to whom you listen to, and wait until you can see clearly for yourself what you need to do.

When you are ready to deal with your financial situation, you will need to review your income and expenditure. If your partner's life was insured, hopefully there will be enough money to repay debt and make up for any shortfall in income. If not, you will need to assess your situation and restructure your assets, liabilities and expenditure so you are in a sustainable position. Your income will need to cover your outgoings, or you will fall deeper and deeper into debt.

Separation and divorce

Separation and divorce can be just as traumatic as the death of a partner, and have even more complications. It is not possible to leave a relationship and suffer no financial consequences, and unwillingness by one or both partners to let go of assets and money often causes considerable distress.

From a financial perspective, there are two key issues to resolve:

- the division of relationship property
- the ongoing financial obligations of each partner to the other.

It is best to try and reach an agreement as quickly as possible. Disputes over division of property can drag on for months or years and incur significant legal costs, as well as potential loss of value for one or both parties. When there is a business involved, property division can be especially complicated as valuations may vary widely.

Once the division of property has been agreed, you will need to prepare a budget based on your new level of assets and income. A difficult issue will be whether or not to keep the family home. While keeping it may be desirable from the point of view of continuity and security for children, it is not always the best decision if you end up with a large mortgage that places a huge burden on your finances and gets you into ever more debt.

Don't forget to update your will.

A separation will not alter the provisions of your existing will. While a new relationship may be the last thing on your mind, it is wise to start thinking about how you can protect your remaining assets in future relationships. Contracting-out agreements and family trusts are two mechanisms by which you can ensure your assets are not further depleted if a subsequent relationship breaks down. It is best to get expert help on this *before* you begin a new relationship, so that you are aware of the financial risks you face and the possible solutions.

Windfall gain

Most of us dream of having a windfall during our lifetime, whether a large inheritance, a lottery win, or the sale of a business for a substantial sum. Sometimes it happens!

Ironically, though, if you are not familiar with handling and investing large amounts of money this can be a frightening and worrying time.

Many people choose to take a conservative approach to managing the money because they are afraid of losing it all. Others see it as an opportunity to spend up large to fulfil lifetime goals.

How you react will be largely determined by your money personality.

Hoarders will want to tuck the money away somewhere safe.

Achievers will relish the thought of being able to buy a mansion and go on a world trip.

Entrepreneurs may buy a business or an investment property.

Thrill-seekers will be tempted to spend it all within a short space of time.

Be guided by the same three rules that apply for the death of a partner.

1. Don't make any significant financial or lifestyle decisions until you feel on an even keel emotionally.
2. Keep your options open.
3. Make your own decisions, but base them on good advice.

Job loss

Losing your job – for whatever reason – can have disastrous implications, particularly if it occurs late in life, when it can be difficult to find alternative employment. You may enter retirement having used up most of your retirement savings for living expenses before becoming eligible for a pension.

If you do get another job, you may take a drop in income. Statistics show that, for most of us, work income peaks when we are in our late forties or early fifties, and thereafter falls quite significantly. Assuming that your income is going to keep increasing during your working life can prove to be a costly mistake.

To reduce the risks posed by potential job loss, always ensure you have an emergency fund, and do not leave your retirement saving until the end of your career.

> **It is unrealistic to plan to do all your retirement saving in the last 10 or 15 years of your working life.**

Birth of a child

Starting a family is a very pleasurable experience, but it can also cause considerable financial stress. If you are used to having two incomes and haven't kept track of your expenditure, it is not always easy to estimate how much you will need to live on when one income is temporarily lost.

The best way to plan for this change is to aim to live on one income for a period of time before you start a family, and save the other income. If you are not able to live on one income before your child is born, you probably won't be able to live on one income afterwards either.

You will also need to reassess your life insurance and income-protection insurance needs, as there will be a period of time when one partner is dependent on the other for either income or childcare. This is also a good time to review your will to ensure your partner and children are well provided for.

Dealing with gradual change

Change can creep up on you. All of a sudden it strikes you that you are not as young as you used to be, your kids are about to leave home, and you would like to work less, or even retire.

Because this happens so gradually, it can take some time to realise that your financial needs and priorities have altered. Things that were important to you when you were young – such as having a car that was the envy of your friends – become less important. Friends and family now mean more than material possessions.

Relationships are a good example of how things can creep up on you. In New Zealand, under the Property (Relationships) Act your partner may be entitled to a share of relationship property once your relationship has lasted three years. Those three years can pass by before you know it, mostly because it is difficult to identify the start of a relationship until you have been in it for some time.

You will also need to consider how you will provide for your partner in the event of your death or illness, and should therefore review your will and your insurances.

Once your children are financially independent – although some parents would argue that this never happens – and you have substantially reduced your mortgage, you may find that your life insurance and income-protection insurance require review: the amount of cover you need could have changed.

As you get older, you may spend more money staying in good health, and so you will need to review your health insurance and, in case you have to reduce your workload, your income-protection insurance.

Estate planning will also take on a more prominent role. The older you are, the more important it is that all your affairs are in order. Your will should be reviewed from time to time, and you should consider granting enduring powers of attorney to someone you trust in the event that you become mentally incapacitated (see page 196).

Retiring or working less

Transition into working less or retiring can be enjoyable, but it can also present some challenges in planning for the future. While you are still working full-time, it is not easy to assess what your living expenses will be when this is not the case. The prospect of a substantial, and possibly sudden, drop in income can be daunting.

A novel but enlightening way of making the transition easier is to get an estimate of the amount of pension income to which you will be entitled, and then try and live on it for a period of time while you are still working, adding a little to cover any costs directly associated with working, such as travel and clothes. You may well go over your budget, but making the transition gradually over a period of time – say, two years or so – will be a lot easier than a sudden change.

Where will you live?

Planning where to live later in life is vital, and mistakes with accommodation can make life miserable. Here are some common ones:

- Using all your retirement savings to buy your dream retirement home, only to find you don't have enough money to live on.
- Buying a 'licence to occupy' in a retirement village, only to find it's not the lifestyle you want.
- Staying in your family home when it needs expensive maintenance, such as painting and re-roofing, that is beyond your budget.
- Planning to get money for living expenses by selling your home and buying a smaller one – only to find that a smaller, modern, maintenance-free house or apartment costs the same or more than your big old family home.

And then there are the success stories. When I first met my client Heather she was in her early sixties and was on a sickness benefit, as she had significant health problems that were likely to get worse. Her poor health severely affected her mobility and she required daily assistance in her home, as well as expensive medical treatment.

Heather had a small amount of savings and was worried about how she was going to afford to live in her retirement. It was unlikely that she would work again, and so she would not be able to add to her savings.

Heather lived in an expensive suburb close to the centre of a large city, in a house that was not well suited to someone with a disability as it was on a hilly site. Looking at options for Heather's future, we decided that it would make sense for her to sell her home and move to a popular retirement area out of town. She was able to buy a comfortable, low-maintenance home with flat access for around $200,000 less than the amount she had received for her city home. We invested this money to provide additional income to cover her expenses, and while Heather still suffers from ill health, she is free from financial worries.

Start creating wealth today!

The best time to start your wealth-creation plan is right now. As you take that first step, remember: seven things will make you succeed.

1. **Know and take account of your money personality.** It is the foundation on which your plans should be made.
2. **Define your guiding principles.** You will know these once you have established the role of money in your life.
3. **Set clear goals** that are consistent with your guiding principles and your money personality, so you are motivated to make necessary changes.
4. **Write down your goals** and your strategies for making them happen.
5. **Systemise your money management using technology** so you manage your money effectively and create wealth automatically.
6. **Take action,** starting in the next 24 hours.
7. **Review your plan** at least once a year and whenever your circumstances change.

You will be truly amazed how simply you can gain control of your money by following the steps outlined in this book. You will then not only be free from financial worries, you will be free to achieve the things in life that are important to you, and to be the person you want to be.

When you control your money you liberate yourself.

8

Where to invest your money

NOW LET'S LOOK IN MORE DETAIL AT DIFFERENT investment options, and how these may (or may not) suit your money personality. As well as the ones you may immediately think of – superannuation, shares or property – there are hundreds more to choose from. Each comes with its own level of risk and return, and some will therefore be better suited to than to others.

So, which investment or combination of investments will work best for you?

To pare things down to their simplest form, you can invest in:

Managed funds, of which there are various types:

- unit trusts (diversified funds, or a portfolio of sector-specific funds)
- superannuation schemes
- listed trusts

Direct investments:

- shares
- fixed-interest investments, such as finance company debentures, corporate bonds and capital notes
- property
- your own business

Your investments may also be a combination of some or all the above.

If you don't have a lump sum to invest but can afford to save a regular amount, you can save by making regular contributions to a managed fund.

If you prefer direct investments but don't have a lump sum, you will need to either borrow funds to invest or save a lump sum in a bank account before investing.

Managed funds

A managed fund consists of a pool of money contributed by various different investors and invested in assets held by an independent trustee on behalf of investors. The assets are managed, for a fee, by a professional fund manager, in accordance with a trust deed that gives guidelines about where and how the funds are to be invested. In theory, as you are using the experience and knowledge of a professional manager, your investments should produce a higher return than the benchmark market return, and this should at least offset the fees paid.

What are the benefits?

There are several benefits to this kind of investment.

- Because funds are pooled, transaction costs such as brokerage are kept to a minimum.
- Investing overseas is considerably easier as the selection and associated paperwork is taken care of by the fund manager.
- You can invest in a market without having to know anything about it, without administrative hassles, and without needing large amounts of capital.

Managed funds are either:

diversified (contain a mix of different asset types), or

sector-specific (invest in only one type of asset – usually cash, fixed interest, property or shares – or one geographic area – for example New Zealand, Australia, or Asia).

You can choose whether you invest in one diversified fund or a number of sector-specific ones. In either case, you need to consider how your total investment is split between the four asset classes – cash, fixed interest, property and shares. This is what financial planners refer to as the asset allocation (see page 169). A diversified fund will have a broadly defined asset allocation that is determined by its trust deed, and the fund manager must keep within those guidelines.

> The fund you choose should have an asset allocation that suits your money personality and feels right for you.

Ultimately, though, the most important decision is not which diversified fund you invest in, but which asset allocation you select.

If you choose to go into sector-specific funds, spread your investment across a range of funds so as to cover each asset class. Remember, it is your asset allocation that will mainly determine the return you get, so set your desired allocation and stick to it. Otherwise, your portfolio may produce more risk than you are comfortable with, or a smaller return.

If you have a small amount to invest, you may be best to choose one diversified fund rather than several sector-specific funds, as you may not be able to meet the minimum investment amounts for the sector-specific funds.

Portfolio Investment Entities (PIEs)

In New Zealand, there is a special type of managed fund called a Portfolio Investment Entity (PIE) that offers tax benefits to investors. To become a PIE, a managed fund must meet certain criteria laid down in legislation. The two principal tax benefits of PIEs are:

1. No capital gains tax for investments in Australasian shares – only income from these investments is taxed.
2. Overseas investments are taxed according to the Fair Dividend Rate (FDR), that is, on 5% of their market value. Most listed Australian shares are exempt from this tax.
3. Investors are taxed at their individual marginal tax rate, which is capped at 30% and based on income from all sources other than PIEs. That means, for example, that an investor on the lowest marginal tax rate can earn income from sources other than PIEs up to the limit of the lowest tax bracket and still be taxed only at the lowest rate on PIE income. For investors on higher rates of marginal tax, there are, therefore, significant tax advantages in investing in PIEs, as opposed to investing directly.

For most investors, there are tax advantages in investing in PIEs rather than other managed funds. PIEs were introduced in October 2007 and many older investment products were not converted to PIEs, or were unable to be converted.

If you invested in a managed fund before October 2007, check to see whether your fund is now a PIE. If it's not, consider reinvesting your funds elsewhere or suspending contributions into it.

There may, of course, be good reasons to retain an investment that is not a PIE. For example, it may include life insurance cover that you may not be able to replace, or that may be replaceable only with very high premiums.

Choosing the fund manager

The way a fund performs will be determined to a large extent by how the manager manages it. You need to consider two questions with regard to the style of management:

- Is the fund manager an active or passive manager?
- If an active manager, what is their investment strategy or philosophy?

Passive management v. active management

A passive fund invests according to a standard formula, which is usually based on a share-market index. The fund imitates the composition of the index, and therefore its performance parallels the performance of the index.

The main advantage of passive funds is that they tend to have lower fees than actively managed funds, as there is little skill or research required to choose the investments.

Passive funds work well when the market is rising, as performance will be good and fees will be low.

However, when the market is falling it can be worthwhile paying higher fees for an actively managed fund, so your investment doesn't fall as much as the market. The skill of an active fund manager lies in being able to pick shares that will perform well despite the overall market trend. A good active fund manager can significantly outperform the market index.

Investment strategy or philosophy

Active fund managers describe themselves as value managers, growth managers or a mixture of the two.

In essence, value managers are bargain hunters. They make an assessment of the fair value of an investment based on current performance and future prospects, and purchase investments they consider to be priced in the market at below the assessed fair value.

A growth manager, on the other hand, will look for investments where, for whatever reason, the future value is expected to rise – even if the current market value may be above the assessed fair value.

Value-managed funds tend to be more stable during times of market volatility, but may underperform growth-managed funds in periods of high growth.

> You can reduce your investment risk by spreading your investments between different fund managers with different styles.

How to choose a managed fund

Ten things you should look at:

- How is the fund taxed – is it a PIE?
- What are the entry/exit fees?
- What are the management fees?
- How good is its track record?
- How big is the fund?
- What is the cost of switching between funds?
- What are the underlying assets in which the fund invests?
- How does the fund deal with foreign currency exposure?
- Are there any restrictions on how funds may be invested by the fund manager?
- What is the management style of the fund manager?

Much of this information will be set out in the fund's investment statement.

Superannuation schemes

Superannuation schemes are a type of managed fund. The difference between them and other types of managed funds, such as unit trusts, lies in how they are taxed. Many superannuation schemes have been converted to Portfolio Investment Entities (PIEs) and are now taxed according to that regime, and this means there is little difference between a superannuation scheme and other PIEs. Superannuation schemes do, however, offer investors the ability to lock in their savings until they reach retirement age. This can be of benefit for thrill-seekers, who may otherwise be tempted to draw on their retirement savings before they retire.

Sometimes employers will offer a superannuation scheme to employees in which the costs are subsidised. The employer may even contribute to the scheme in proportion to the employee's contribution, and this kind of scheme may be offered as an alternative to KiwiSaver (see pages 227–230). In many cases, employer schemes that are KiwiSaver-compliant may offer superior benefits to a standard KiwiSaver scheme – in other words, you will have all the benefits of KiwiSaver and more.

Superannuation schemes are professionally managed, and most offer flexibility in how your funds are invested: you can change the investment mix over time as your requirements change.

Once you have chosen a superannuation scheme you will need to choose your investment option within the scheme. That means selecting a diversified fund with an asset allocation that suits your money personality, or a range of sector-specific funds that give you a customised asset allocation.

How to choose a superannuation scheme

There are hundreds of schemes to choose from. Shop around before you decide. These are useful questions to ask.

- Is this scheme a PIE (Portfolio Investment Entity)?
- Is this a Registered Superannuation Scheme?
- Who is the fund manager? Is there just one, or several?
- What has its performance been, compared to other similar schemes?
- What are the entry/exit and switching fees?
- What are the management fees?
- Will my funds be locked in until retirement age?
- How flexible is the scheme in terms of changes to the investment mix and contributions?
- How big is the scheme?

KiwiSaver

In New Zealand, KiwiSaver was introduced on 1 July 2007 to give taxpayers a simple, cost-effective way to save for retirement or a first home. A KiwiSaver scheme is a diversified managed fund that meets certain criteria and has been approved as a KiwiSaver scheme. Information on KiwiSaver and a lost of approved KiwiSaver schemes can be found on *www.kiwisaver.govt.nz.* You can join KiwiSaver if you are under the age of 65. You do not have to be in employment, and children and self-employed people can join.

> Most eligible people should join KiwiSaver.

The principal reason for not joining would be if, for some reason, you can't reduce your expenditure to a level where you can afford to make the minimum contribution. For KiwiSavers joining through their employer, the minimum contribution is 4% of pay, and for KiwiSavers joining directly with a scheme provider, the minimum contribution is set by the scheme provider.

KiwiSaver is attractive because of the compulsory employer contributions and the tax credits.

- **Compulsory employer contributions** start at 1% of pay from 1 April 2008, and increase by 1% each year to a maximum of 4% by 1 April 2011. Your employer will receive a tax credit of up to $20 per week towards your employer contribution and there will be no withholding tax paid on employer contributions.
- **A tax credit** of up to $20 a week ($1,042 a year) will be paid into your KiwiSaver account, along with a fee rebate of $40 a year. There is also an initial government contribution of $1,000 when you join. If you are self-employed or not working (for example, you are at home looking after children or have retired early), you will still be able get the tax credits, which will be paid directly into your KiwiSaver account. The amount of the tax credit matches the contribution, so to get the maximum you will need to contribute at least $20 a week.

Self-employed people whose business is operated through a company, trust or partnership, and who are paid a salary or wage with PAYE deductions, can join KiwiSaver as an employee of their business, and in that way can be paid an employer contribution by the business. The benefit of this arrangement is that there is no withholding tax paid on the employer contribution and there is also a tax credit of $20 per week paid to the business by the government towards the employer contribution. Self-employed people on the highest marginal tax rate should give serious consideration to taking advantage of these tax benefits.

For information on how KiwiSaver will work for you, click on the Quick KiwiSaver calculator at *www.sorted.org.nz*. By simply entering your age, your annual pay and the frequency of your pay, you will see the benefits you will gain.

Your funds will be locked in until you reach retirement age, unless special conditions apply, such as as purchasing your first home, permanent emigration or financial hardship. However, you can switch from one KiwiSaver scheme to another.

KiwiSavers with household incomes below a certain level may be eligible for a first-home deposit subsidy, subject to certain conditions. You may also be able to divert up to half of your contributions to your mortgage after the first year.

KiwiSaver should be your first choice for retirement saving because of the employer subsidies and government tax credits. However, don't make the mistake of thinking that if you join KiwiSaver you don't need to worry about any other form of saving for retirement. Calculate your total contribution to KiwiSaver, including your contribution, your employer's contribution and the tax credits. Compare this with what you calculated as the annual saving you need to do to reach your retirement goals, as set out in Step 3 on page 96. If it's not enough, you will need to need to have additional retirement savings elsewhere, for example through a diversified managed fund or a superannuation scheme.

KiwiSaver is, essentially, just a special type of diversified managed fund. Each provider has to have a selection of investment options available, ranging from conservative to aggressive, based on how investments are allocated between shares, property and fixed interest. If you join

KiwiSaver but do not choose a provider, or if you choose a provider but not choose an investment option, you will be put into a default fund, which will be conservative. This may not be in your best long-term interest and may not suit your money personality.

> With KiwiSaver, it is very important that you choose both a provider and an investment option.

How to choose a KiwiSaver scheme

Here are some useful questions to ask.

- Who is the fund manager? Is there just one, or several?
- What has its performance been, compared with other similar schemes?
- What are the management fees?
- What are the exit and switching fees?
- Does the fund cover all asset classes?
- How flexible is the scheme in terms of changing the investment mix?
- How big is the scheme?
- Does the scheme offer mortgage diversion?

Once you have selected a provider, your most important decision will be selecting which fund within the scheme to invest in. There will usually be a selection of diversified funds, with labels such as 'conservative', 'balanced' and 'aggressive'. Each of these will have a mix of cash, fixed interest, property and shares. The difference will be in the asset allocation. While each will have a small amount invested in cash and property, a conservative fund will be more heavily invested in fixed interest and an aggressive fund in shares. A balanced fund will be roughly equally invested between fixed interest and shares.

You should select the diversified fund that most closely fits your money personality. By now you will have analysed your personality, and have a good idea of how bold you can and should be. Hoarders will have a natural preference for a conservative fund that will increase in value slowly but steadily. Entrepreneurs will have a tendency for aggressive funds that potentially produce a high return but with considerable risk, orvolatility. Achievers tend to opt for balanced funds as they weigh up their desire for wealth against their natural conservative tendencies, while thrill-seekers, if they invest at all, are comfortable with a fund that is anywhere between balanced and aggressive.

Some KiwiSaver schemes also have a choice of sector-specific funds. For example, there may be an Australasian share fund, an international share fund, a property fund and a fixed interest fund. If this is the case, instead of selecting a diversified fund you can spread your investment over a number of sector-specific funds. For example, you may allocate 25% to a fixed interest fund, 5% to a property fund, 30% to Australasian shares, and 40% to international shares. You are able to customise the asset allocation to your own needs, and modify it over time.

Listed trusts

A listed trust is another type of managed fund. However, it is what is referred to as a 'closed' fund. It has a company structure, with a given number of shares that are traded on the share market. The value of the shares is determined by the value of the company's underlying investments – for instance, its shares in other companies – and the trends in the share market as a whole.

This means that investing in a listed trust can carry a double whammy. When the share market as a whole is showing strong growth, the shares in the listed trust may increase, due to both the rise in value of the underlying investments and the upward trend in the share market.

In this situation, returns from listed trusts can be higher than the increase in value of the underlying investments.

Conversely, though, if the share market heads downwards, the value of shares in the listed trust can fall more than the value of the underlying investments.

Listed trusts often have a particular investment focus – for example, commercial and industrial property, New Zealand shares, Australian shares, international shares, pharmaceutical companies and infrastructure companies.

Evaluating the performance of managed funds

With the share-market downturn of 2000 to 2003, managed funds lost a lot of credibility with investors. Many investors – and ill-informed commentators – failed to understand that the reason for the poor performance of many managed funds was simply the poor performance of the share market.

The benchmark against which the performance of a fund manager should be assessed is the index relevant to the market in which the fund is invested: there is a limit to how much value a fund manager can add. When a market is falling by 20%, it is unreasonable to expect a fund based on the market to increase in value. The performance will be within a small margin of the performance of the market. For example, if the international share market index were to fall by 20% in a given period, a managed fund based on international shares that fell by only 15% after fees over the same period could be considered to be performing well: it is outperforming the index.

It is not appropriate to measure the short-term performance of managed funds against bank deposit rates. In the short term (that is, periods of less than five to ten years) performance should be measured against the market index for the asset class, or against a portfolio of direct investments from the same asset class. However, it is reasonable to expect managed funds to outperform bank deposit rates over the long term.

If you have a small amount to invest, or want to invest offshore, you will substantially reduce your risk if you invest in an actively managed fund, where your money will be spread across many different shares that have been selected by informed experts. Choose a fund that has a track record of outperforming the market index.

> Managed funds are ideal for conservative investors such as hoarders and achievers, as they usually involve less risk than directly investing in the same types of assets.

How safe is my money in a managed fund?

This is a common question my clients ask. The issues here are:

- What happens if the fund manager goes broke?
- Is putting all your money into one managed fund the same as having all your eggs in one basket?

The key point is that the fund manager does not own the investments being managed. They are held by a trustee on your behalf. The trustee's role is to ensure that funds are being invested in accordance with the trust deed, and the trustee appoints the fund manager to make investment decisions.

A fund manager is in the business of managing funds for other people, in a similar way to a property manager who purchases and looks after a rental property on behalf of an investor. If the fund manager strikes financial difficulties within its own business and has to cease operating, the trustee may be forced to hire a new fund manager but your investments will stay intact.

The risks you take with a managed fund are twofold.

1 The investment markets in which your money is invested could fall. This can be managed by ensuring your money is spread across all the different asset classes, either in a diversified fund or in several sector-specific funds.

2 Your fund manager may make poor investment decisions. This can be managed by putting your money in a fund that uses several different fund managers, or in several different managed funds with different managers.

Direct investments

If you are an **entrepreneur** or a **thrill-seeker**, you will probably prefer to invest directly, rather than use the expertise of a fund manager. Direct investments, particularly in property and shares, offer the prospect of high returns for investors with the ability to spot the opportunities and the courage to act on them.

Hoarders and **achievers** are not generally included in that category, but this doesn't mean they shouldn't invest directly. If you are a hoarder or an achiever, your direct investments will be less risky because you are likely to have done some careful research.

Shares

The principal advantage of investing in shares directly, rather than through a managed fund, is that you save on fees. Some investors also have an active interest in shares, enjoy following share-market prices and information, and find there is more satisfaction in investing directly.

To invest successfully you will need a reasonably large amount of money so you can spread yourself across a number of different shares. You will need to ensure your portfolio is diversified by industry group, with a mix of investments in 'blue chip' (solid, mature companies with a proven track record) and 'blue sky' (new or high growth companies that are yet to be proven).

If you need income from your portfolio, choose shares that have a policy of high dividend payments. If you are already on a high income – and therefore a high marginal tax rate – it may be best for you to choose shares that have low dividends but high growth in value.

It is always a good idea to seek advice from an expert, such as a share-broker or financial adviser. Whatever you do, don't rely on 'hot tips' from friends and acquaintances. Do your own research, talk to experts and come to your own conclusions.

The New Zealand Stock Exchange website, *www.nzx.com*, has some useful information for first-time investors. Familiarise yourself with the jargon of the share market, and read up as much as you can about the companies in which you intend to invest. It is useful to have some basic accounting knowledge so you can make sense of company annual reports, and you can also take evening classes in share investing. Setting up a share club with friends is another way of sharing knowledge.

If you haven't a clue where to start, are not really interested in shares or don't have time to do the research, you are probably better off investing in shares through a managed fund.

Fixed-interest investments

Other than bank deposits, the main types of fixed-interest investments are:

- finance company debentures and notes
- corporate bonds and notes

With fixed-interest investments, you need to carefully compare the risk you are taking with the likely return. It's the old story of high return means high risk – but with some fixed-interest investments a high return may not be enough to compensate for an even higher level of risk.

Diversification is just as important in fixed-interest investments as it is with shares.

> Don't put all your money with one company.

Finance company debentures

Finance companies lend money on property, vehicles, and plant and equipment, or on retail goods such as whiteware and furniture. Usually they specialise in one of these categories.

There are a myriad of finance companies and often they don't have a long life span, so investing in this sector needs particularly careful scrutiny – both of the company itself and the people advising you to invest in it.

In New Zealand it is proposed that from 2009 all finance companies over a certain size will be required to have a rating, and those that are under the threshold will need to advertise the fact that they are not rated. You should ensure that the rating of the finance company is 'investment grade'. Each rating company will have a different rating scale, so familiarise yourself with what is considered to be investment grade.

How to decide whether to invest with a finance company

Some of the things you should always look at before investing with a finance company:

- What is its rating?
- How big is the company? (What are its total assets?)
- How long has it been in business?
- Who are the people behind it and what is their track record?
- What type of lending does it do?
- Does it lend money to related parties (for example, to a parent or subsidiary company)?
- What is the level of shareholders' funds?
- What is the company's track record on bad debts?
- Has it made adequate provision for bad debts?

Corporate bonds and capital notes

Simply put, corporate bonds are securities issued by large companies. These organisations issue securities direct to investors, rather than borrowing from a bank, because it lowers their borrowing costs.

Some companies also issue **capital notes**, which have a lower level of security than bonds and therefore usually offer a higher rate of interest.

The New Zealand government also issues bonds and these are referred to as government stock. Because government stock is such low risk, it offers a low return.

There is a secondary market for corporate bonds and notes: after being issued, they can be bought and sold at prices that may be different from their face value. The price is determined by the perceived risk of the investment and the prevailing market interest rates. In general, a bond or note paying an interest rate above market rates will sell at a premium *above* its face value; a bond or note paying an interest rate below market rates will sell at *less* than its face value. As the bond gets closer to its maturity date the premium or discount will become lower, and will disappear at maturity.

Most bonds and notes mature at least five years from the date of issue, and are bought or sold through a sharebroker. While in theory they are fixed-interest investments, there is an increasing trend for notes with longer maturities, and perpetual notes, to have resettable interest rates. Hence, the rate can vary up or down as market interest rates change.

Most bonds and some notes come with a Standard & Poor's rating: a rating of BBB– and above is considered to be investment grade.

Property investment

At least 70 percent of New Zealanders aspire to own their own home. As a result, the country has one of the highest rates of home ownership in the world. Perhaps our love affair with property can be traced back to our colonial roots – our ancestors were so keen to have their own piece of land they risked their lives and endured harsh living conditions to make it a reality.

For most people, property is a comfortable investment. We can choose to live in the property ourselves or let it. We can touch it, admire it and show it off to our friends. And we can use it as security for a loan. There is also the popular belief that land must be a good investment because they're not making any more of it. It is not surprising, then, that when New Zealanders set about creating wealth or establishing a retirement fund, property investment is often top of the list.

> Your own home is not an investment.

Money tied up in a home does not produce a return. And while your home may increase in value, the cash will be available only if you sell it and buy something cheaper – and most people find it difficult to drop their standard of living.

To maximise your wealth-creation opportunities, ideally you should live in the lowest cost house in which you feel comfortable. If you are renting because you enjoy the flexibility of being a tenant, consider buying an investment property to ensure you have a foot in the property sector. Otherwise you may find that later in life, when you want to purchase a house, prices may have moved beyond your means.

Investing in property is gaining in popularity, driven by:

- rising property prices
- the prospect of big capital gains, and
- an increase in the number of people renting.

One of the reasons property works so well as an investment is that it is usually leveraged – that is, it relies on borrowed funds rather than your own. It is possible to earn a large amount, provided the return on the investment is greater than the cost of borrowing and other expenses associated with maintaining the property.

Investing in property is a numbers game. Unless you know how to calculate the overall return you will get, you run a real risk of buying a property that won't be a good investment.

Return from a property investment

There are two parts to the return from property – income and capital gain. Income can be looked at as either a gross or net amount.

Gross income yield = the total income per year, divided by the value of the property.

Net income yield = the income after you have deducted expenses and tax, divided by the value of the property.

As a general rule:

- Properties with high potential for capital gain produce a low net income yield.
- Properties with high net income yield have low potential for capital gain.

This is because rent does not go up in proportion to the value of the house. For example, a three-bedroom house valued at $150,000 may rent for $200 a week, whereas a three-bedroom house valued at $300,000 may rent for $250 a week.

From the point of view of income yield, it is better to own two houses, each valued at $150,000 and producing combined rent of $400 per week, than to own one house valued at $300,000 and producing $250 per week.

However, you also need to take capital gain into account: it may be that the potential for capital gain is much higher for the $300,000 property. To make a comparison between the two options, calculate the combined income yield and capital gain for each (see the section below on calculating the return).

Before you start building a property portfolio, decide on your investment strategy.

Are you investing for high capital gain or high income? Or are you hoping to find a property where you can achieve both?

The advantage of investing for high capital gain – providing you are not deemed by the tax department to be in the business of buying and selling properties – is that the capital gain you make on the eventual sale of your property may not be taxable.

The disadvantage is that you won't get the capital gain until the property is sold. In the meantime, the low income yield may not cover your expenses, and you may have to contribute money from your own pocket each week towards the mortgage.

The disadvantage of investing for high income yield is that your property, which probably came cheap because of its location or condition, may not increase much in value, and/or may require expensive maintenance. Also, the income will be taxable. Conversely, if you have done your homework well the income should be sufficient to meet the outgoings.

Occasionally a property will both produce a high income yield *and* have potential for high capital gain. This can happen when:

- You purchase a property significantly below its market value. You may be able to do this if:
  - the seller needs a quick sale, or
  - minor modifications – for example, adding a fence or a garage, or creating additional bedrooms – will substantially improve the property's value.
- Prices in the area are poised to grow significantly because of economic factors such as growth in a local industry, population increase, or just a catch-up with the national average.

How to calculate the return

The simplest way to evaluate whether a property will produce a good enough return is to do a very basic calculation of annual income and outgoings.

1. **Calculate the gross income**. This will be the weekly rent multiplied by the number of weeks in the year for which the property will be rented. You should allow around four weeks per year for vacancy.

   If you are not familiar with market rents in the area, ask a local property manager to do a rent appraisal. Market rents in different areas are available on rental agency websites and, in New Zealand, on the Tenancy Services website *www.dbh.govt.nz/tenancy*.

2. **Add up the outgoings**. These will include:
   - mortgage repayments
   - rates
   - insurance
   - maintenance
   - property management fee (optional)
   - lawn and garden care (optional).

3. **Deduct total outgoings from total income**. This will give you the net annual cash flow before tax from the property. If it is a positive number, the property will put money in your bank. If it is negative, you will have to put in your own money to cover the shortfall.

The effect of tax

This simple analysis does not include tax. For tax purposes, you cannot claim repayments of principal as an expense, but you can claim interest.

You can also claim depreciation on the house and chattels. If the amount of depreciation is *more* than the cash surplus, or there is a cash shortfall, you will have a tax loss that can be offset against your other income. If the amount of depreciation is *less* than the cash surplus, you will have to pay tax on the difference.

Try these shortcuts

If you intend to borrow to buy a property and don't want to put in your own money to cover the outgoings, here are simple methods you can use to help find a suitable property.

1. Calculate the gross income yield on each property. This is the weekly rent multiplied by 48 (allowing for four weeks' vacancy), divided by the value of the property. For example, a property with a purchase price of $200,000 and a weekly rent of $250 has a gross yield of 250 x 48 ÷ 200,000 or 6%.

   Outgoings, apart from interest, will comprise 1.5% to 3.5% of the value of the property, depending how much maintenance is required. This means that if you are paying more than 4.5% interest, the property will have a cash flow shortfall (negative cash flow).

2. Alternatively, start with how much it will cost you to borrow money. If you are paying 6.5% interest, you will need a gross income yield of at least 8% to have a neutral cash flow.

This analysis ignores the tax benefits of depreciation allowances, but it is not a good idea to rely on tax benefits to make an investment worthwhile – with changes in government policy they can be here today and gone tomorrow.

And as I've already mentioned, when you sell your property the tax department may claw-back any tax benefit you have earned through claiming depreciation.

How to decide on the best property to buy

This table compares a property with a cash surplus (positive cash flow) with a property with a cash shortfall (negative cash flow). The property with the positive cash flow was purchased for $100,000, while the negative cash-flow property was purchased for $200,000.

Annual income and outgoings	Positive cash-flow property purchased for for $100,000	Negative cash-flow property purchased for for $200,000
A – Income: rent	$11,000	$12,500
B – Outgoings		
Interest (interest-only mortgage)	$6,500	$13,000
Rates	$1,200	$1,800
Insurance	$300	$500
Maintenance	$2,000	$2,000
Total outgoings	$10,000	$17,300
C – Net cash flow before tax (A minus B)	$1,000	($4,800)
Less depreciation	($3,000)	($6,000)
Profit/loss before tax	($2,000)	($10,800)
D – Tax to pay (or refund) at 33%	Refund of $660	Refund of $3,564
E – Net cash flow after tax (C plus D)	$1,660	($1,236)

Because you can claim depreciation for tax purposes but don't have to pay for it in hard cash, the after-tax cash flow is a net *inflow* of $1,660 for the positive cash-flow property, while the after-tax cash flow for the negative cash-flow property is a net cash *outflow* of $1,236.

Which is the better investment?

To assess which property would make the better investment, calculate the net income yield for each and add the estimated capital gain.

F – Property value	$100,000	$200,000
Cash-flow yield (E divided by F)	1.67%	-0.62%
Estimated capital gain (%)	5.00%	7.00%
Total return	6.67%	6.38%

Based on the assumptions made, you will get a slightly better return from the positive cash-flow property. However, this doesn't mean that all positive cash-flow properties produce a better return.

This analysis is highly simplified, and does not take into account that, when you sell your property, you may have to pay back to the tax department the tax benefit you have received from claiming depreciation.

Another aspect to consider is that a negative cash-flow property will be a drain on your cash resources, and you will need to sell the property to realise your return. However, since rents gradually rise over time, a negative cash-flow property will become positive cash-flow at some point.

> Always do a full analysis of all properties you are considering buying to judge which will give you the best return.

More complex analysis

An alternative to this simple analysis is to prepare a spreadsheet that looks at how the properties you're considering would perform over, say, a ten-year period. This way you will take into consideration one-off maintenance costs, such as painting and re-roofing, and more accurately assess the amount of depreciation you can claim each year, which will progressively diminish. Specialist books on property investment – for example, *Building Wealth through Investment Property* by Dolf de Roos and Jan Somers – give further guidance on how to do this analysis.

Next, decide what you would consider to be an adequate yield on your investment. Consider only those properties that you expect will meet or exceed your benchmark. Finding such properties may require considerable time and effort; many properties will be appealing but not stack up as investments.

How to increase income yield

There are many ways to increase a property's income yield. You can follow the now-common practice of renting it out room by room, rather than as a whole. You can convert living rooms into bedrooms, add another dwelling to the site, or refurbish the property so it commands a higher rent.

Despite this, your purchase decision should always be made on an 'as is' basis. You will often see investment properties advertised as 'currently rented for $xxx per week but potential to increase'. The price you pay for such a property should be based on the current rent, not potential future rent that is, of course, far from guaranteed.

Ownership and financing of your investment property

Ownership options include for an investment property include:

- individual ownership
- joint ownership
- tenants in common
- company
- LAQC (Loss Attributing Qualifying Company)
- family trust.

Seek advice from an accountant or solicitor as to which option is the most appropriate for you. Each has different advantages and disadvantages for tax, estate planning and asset protection – for example, you may decide to put a loss-making property into a family trust because protecting your assets is more important than getting immediate access to tax benefits.

If you have, or intend to have, a family trust there are two key pitfalls to be aware of. The first is that if you transfer the ownership of an investment property from you to your family trust, this is in effect a sale of your property and will trigger depreciation claw-back: you will need to pay back the tax benefit you have claimed from depreciation.

The second pitfall is that if an investment property running at a tax loss is owned by your family trust, you will not be able to use the losses unless or until the trust has enough other income against which the loss can be offset. This may mean waiting several years until the property is running at a tax profit, at which time the losses from previous years can be carried forward to reduce the amount of tax you pay.

> If you want to make immediate use of tax benefits, consider setting up a LAQC.

An LAQC is a special type of company in which tax losses can be passed through to shareholders to offset against their personal income. Once the property is running at a profit the shares can be sold to your family trust, so the property is then protected by the trust. Because the shares in the property-owning company, rather than the property itself, are sold to the trust, this sale should not trigger depreciation claw-back.

How to structure your mortgage

It's important to structure your mortgage with care, to ensure you can deduct interest payments against your investment income. Again, professional advice will be useful. Whether interest is tax-deductible depends on the purpose for which the borrowing was undertaken. For example, if you borrow $200,000 to buy an investment property and the loan is secured by way of a mortgage over both the investment property and your own residence, then the purpose of the mortgage is to buy the investment property, and the interest on the borrowing will be deductible against the rental income.

If, on the other hand, you borrow $200,000 to purchase a new house for yourself and then put tenants into your existing home, the purpose of the mortgage is to buy a house for yourself and the interest will probably not be deductible against the income from the rental property. This situation can be overcome with expert advice.

Providing the mortgage on your investment property is tax-deductible, you can optimise your tax benefits by making it interest-only. As well as this, though, you should set aside the money you would have used to pay off principal on your investment loan to pay off the mortgage on your family home (which is not tax-deductible).

If you don't have a mortgage on your home, save the equivalent of the principal payments into a diversified managed fund or another investment of your choice. Then, when you want your investment property to be debt-free, you can cash up your managed fund or other investments to repay the mortgage. This strategy will work well providing the after-tax return on your investments is equal to, or greater than, the after-tax cost of interest on your mortgage.

The reason for using an interest-only mortgage is obvious when you do some simple calculations. Let's say you have borrowed money at 6% for your investment property. The interest is tax-deductible. Therefore, if you are on a 33% tax rate, the net cost to you is only 4% (that is, 67% of 6%). If you pay back the principal on this mortgage, you will, in effect, be 'earning' only 4% on your money. If you have a mortgage on your family home that is greater than 4%, you will 'earn' more from your money by using it to repay that mortgage.

Alternatively, you should be able to achieve a net return of at least 4% after tax by saving into a diversified fund. Should you wish to repay the mortgage on your investment property you can cash up the fund.

Getting advice

A very important step is to familiarise yourself with tenancy law – such as, in New Zealand, the Residential Tenancies Act – and your obligations and rights as a landlord.

CASE STUDY

One well-known New Zealand property investor started investing in property when he was 24, and by his mid thirties had created wealth of more than $1 million.

He started by buying a home for himself and bringing in flatmates. Realising there was money in being a landlord, he then bought two rental properties in a low-value suburb. However, he soon found that because of their location they attracted the wrong kind of tenants.

He started learning as much about property investment as he could by reading and attending seminars, and then began a new strategy of buying and renovating. Some houses he keeps, but most he sells for a quick profit. His strategy is to buy cheaply and renovate and sell within three months, on the basis that the more quickly he turns over the properties the more money he will make.

He deals mostly in low-value properties and prefers to purchase privately from people who are highly motivated to sell. He has lost count of the number of properties he has bought and sold. His focus is on the numbers – how much can he buy it for, what will the renovations cost, and what is the expected resale value? He doesn't always get it right, and as a property trader he is subject to tax on his profits, but he still makes a lot of money.

CASE STUDY **PROPERTY INVESTMENT**

When you purchase an investment property, also purchase a copy of relevant legislation and study it. In New Zealand, there is more information at *www.dbh.govt.nz/tenancy*.

I also recommend tapping into the knowledge of seasoned investors. In New Zealand, there are Property Investors' Associations throughout the country, under the umbrella of the Property Investors' Federation (*www.nzpif.org.nz*). These associations hold monthly meetings that offer both expert advice from guest speakers and the opportunity to rub shoulders with people who have been in the game for decades.

If you do your homework, property can be a solid basis for your investment portfolio. By buying properties below market value, where you can achieve good capital gain in the short term, or properties where minor improvements can add significant value, you will be able to grow your portfolio quite quickly, using the equity as a deposit on more properties – providing you meet your lender's criteria on the loan-to-value ratio, and the percentage of your income that is committed to finance costs.

A good strategy for a beginner

It's good to start by building up a portfolio of several positive cash-flow properties, and then purchasing a negative cash-flow property that can be financed from your positive cash flow. This will give your overall portfolio a balance between income yield and capital gain.

Here's an illustration of how you might build up a portfolio.

Year 1

- Purchase a property for $200,000 – 15% below market value – with a positive cash flow of $2,000 per annum. Interest-only mortgage of $160,000 (80% of property value).
- After six months and some minor redecoration, the property is revalued for lending purposes at $240,000. Equity of $80,000 can now support a mortgage of $320,000.
- Purchase additional property below market value for $160,000, using the equity as the deposit.

Year 2

- The combined value of the properties is now $450,000, with mortgages totalling $320,000, equity of $130,000 and positive cash flow of $5,000 a year.
- Purchase a block of flats below market value for $500,000, using the equity on existing properties as the deposit.

Year 3

- Your properties are now valued at $1,070,000, with mortgages of $820,000, equity of $250,000 and positive cash flow of $15,000 a year.
- Purchase a negative-cash-flow property at market value for $400,000. Finance this using equity as a deposit, and existing positive cash flow to support negative cash flow.

Of course, this is a theoretical example and assumes that properties are available below market value, lenders are willing to make funds available, and property prices rise. However, even though the actual time span may be a little longer if any of these assumptions are not met, the principle remains valid.

Listed property trusts and managed property funds

Two alternatives to investing in property directly are listed property trusts and managed property funds.

Listed property trusts are investment vehicles that are listed on the stock exchange. They raise funds from investors, and pool them to purchase a diversified portfolio of investment properties. The value of the investment is determined by a combination of the value of the underlying property assets and the dynamics of the share market.

These trusts usually pay excellent dividends to investors and are a good source of retirement income: if you need cash quickly you can sell your holding on the share market.

Managed property funds, of which there are many available, operate in a similar way, except that they are not listed and the value of the investment is determined by the value of the underlying assets, rather than being influenced directly by the share market.

Both managed property funds and listed property trusts provide good income streams, with the prospect of capital gain – and, best of all, no midnight calls to fix the plumbing.

Your own business

Many people dream of having their own business, yet few people ever try going into business, and even fewer are successful. Of all money personalities, entrepreneurs are the most attracted to business ownership. They are risk-takers with the passion to succeed.

If you are setting up a business, the biggest challenge is to come up with an idea that is going to work. Start by making a list of things in which you:

- have an interest
- have appropriate strengths, such as skills, knowledge and experience, and
- feel passionate about.

If you love the outdoors, you may make a success of an adventure tourism business.

If you have a flair for colour and design, you could consider a home décor business.

If you are a trained nurse, you could take advantage of the huge growth in aged care to set up a home-based aged-care agency, or a rest home.

If your skills are in management or business development, you could set up a business venture where you will employ people with technical expertise, while you are in charge of sales, marketing and management.

Next, consider the potential market. You may think you have a good idea for a business but will people be willing to pay for the product or service at the price you will need to charge? Do some market research with potential customers, and if possible test the market in a small way before you invest a lot of money.

Your business has to be driven by what customers want. However, needs and wants are often intangible, and extend beyond the product or service itself. For example, cafés don't just sell coffee – they sell an environment in which people relax, feel good and enjoy time with their friends and business acquaintances. It's not enough to produce good coffee and delicious food: your café will need to be in a location that is convenient for people to meet, and have ambience – the right décor and music.

Look at overseas trends and business ideas to identify new opportunities for the local market, but be careful too: what is a success in one market may be a failure in another because of different buyer preferences.

How to come up with a successful business idea

1. Make a list of all the things you are passionate about.
2. Brainstorm ideas for turning these into business opportunities.
3. List your personal strengths and weaknesses.
4. Write down how you can use your strengths in the business opportunities you've identified.
5. Honestly assess how you would deal with your weaknesses.

If you don't want to take the risk of coming up with an entirely new business, there are two other options. You can buy an existing business or you can buy a franchise.

CASE STUDY

In 1999, I decided to move from a general management role into my own business. My story has been documented in the book *You Don't Make a Big Leap without a Gulp* by Mike Fitzsimons and Nigel Beckford (Beckford Publishing), which is all about mid-life career change.

Having worked most of my life in large companies with bureaucratic structures, I wanted the freedom to do my own thing. I started by trying to find a business opportunity that would really motivate me, as well as having a high potential for growth. I had qualifications in economics and accounting and a background in financial services, so something to do with money seemed to be an obvious choice.

I love working with people, so I set about looking for something that involved both money and people. An advertisement for a franchise opportunity in financial planning caught my eye. On doing further research I discovered that the financial planning industry was growing rapidly and there was a huge shortage of qualified people.

Clients were mostly high net-worth retirees, so I set up my business in an area with a high percentage of such people. I had begun my quest for a business opportunity with a vague idea and by following my passion and doing my homework I was able to achieve greater clarity of my vision – to become internationally recognised as a financial planner helping people to have a rich and happy life.

CASE STUDY **BUSINESS OWNERSHIP**

Franchising

Franchising is increasingly popular, although with a successful franchise there is more money to be made as the franchisor – the person or company selling the franchises – than the franchisee.

Before you purchase a franchise, look carefully at what you are getting for your money. There will usually be a substantial initial lump-sum payment and an ongoing fee – either a percentage of turnover or a flat yearly amount. The initial lump sum often purchases start-up stock and equipment and initial training, but will also include an amount that is purely goodwill for the use of the brand and the relevant manuals and systems.

The ongoing franchise fee should be related to the amount of support the franchisor is going to give you with training, management, product supply and the generation of new business. Without this support, you might as well be in business for yourself, without the need to pay franchise fees.

As a franchisee, the resale value of your business will be pegged to the price of other franchises within the business. The value of the brand will depend on the popularity of the product or service, and the amount of marketing and publicity the franchisor undertakes.

With a new franchise, you need to be completely sure the brand will indeed have some value before you pay goodwill for it.

Important questions to ask:

- How many other franchises are going to be sold?
- Will I have exclusive rights for a particular geographic area?
- Is there a 'restraint of trade' that will prevent me setting up in competition if I sell my franchise?

Promotional material for franchise sales often includes financial projections that show exciting-looking profits. Never take these projections at face value. Check the assumptions that lie behind them to see if they are realistic, and speak to existing franchisees about how the business has turned out for them.

Buying a business

Buying an existing business can be a good way to start your business empire. If you are an achiever or a hoarder, buying a business with proven returns is a way of taking a step out of your comfort zone.

Look for a business that has performed poorly due to bad management, or one where you can see potential to add new products and services. You may also consider purchasing several similar businesses and combining them for increased efficiency.

The main risk with buying an existing business is that you will pay too much for it. Business valuation is more of an art than a science and there are several methods. You should get professional advice from an accountant and solicitor before you proceed.

You will need to go through a process of 'due diligence', with the aim of uncovering all the potential risks involved with the business. Looking at the accounts for the last few years is a starting point, but you will also need to uncover risks around the customer base, the product or service, the market and the regulatory environment.

For example, the business may be dependent on one large customer for over half of its revenue. How likely is it that the customer will remain loyal in the future? Is the product or service technology likely to be superseded by competitors? Are new regulations about to be introduced that could increase or decrease the size of the market?

Are you suited to be in business?

Whether you are setting up a new business or buying an existing one, before you take that big leap out of regular paid employment run down this checklist to see if you are really suited to being in business.

1. Is this a business that suits your interests, skills and experience, so you will stay motivated and not need to spend too much time getting up to speed?
2. Are you prepared to work long hours without the security of a regular pay cheque?

3. Do you have a lump sum of money or an alternative income stream to support you while you are getting established?
4. Are you ready and able to learn new skills? As a small business owner, you may have to be managing director, human resources manager, marketing manager, financial controller and production manager, among other things.
5. Do you have a network of people on whom you can call for advice and support?
6. Are you prepared to do whatever it takes to make your business succeed? This may mean not only working long hours, but juggling a variety of roles, going without holidays, undertaking public speaking, making cold calls, dealing with difficult customers, completing tax returns and numerous other tasks.

The business plan

Before you set up your business, it can be a good idea to prepare a business plan. This will document your business idea, your product or service, the potential buyers, the resources you will need, and how you will go about marketing the product or service.

Many businesses fail because they don't have enough capital to get through the difficult early years. To avoid this pitfall, make sure you prepare a budget and cash flow forecast that shows the funding you will require. If you don't know how to do this, get assistance from someone who does, such as an accountant or another business owner who is willing to help you.

> It can take up to five years for a business to become profitable.

Make sure you have sufficient funds to last through this establishment period, and don't give up if you don't make a profit in your first year.

How to write your business plan

Vision

Describe your long-term vision for your business: the products or services you intend to provide, to whom, and how you aim to be different from your competitors.

Rather than a single statement, try writing a description of your business as it will be in, say, ten years' time. Try to put in lots of detail, and focus on what it is that will make your business unique and successful.

Strengths, weaknesses, opportunities and threats (SWOT)

Now focus on your current situation. What are the key strengths of your business? The key weaknesses? What specific business opportunities can you see in the market? What threats will you face from competitors, from changes in the economic environment, or from anything else?

Keys to success

List the things you *must* get right for your business to succeed. Do you have to find the right location? Secure an agreement with a supplier or an important potential customer? Find skilled and experienced staff? Secure a good credit line with a bank at affordable interest?

Goals

Set some specific goals that are measurable and time-bound. These should cover the critical areas of your business, such as sales or market share, personnel, suppliers, customer satisfaction, profit and product development.

Strategies

Identify the strategies you need to achieve these goals. They should be based on your SWOT analysis – building on your strengths and opportunities and addressing your weaknesses and threats.

Actions

For each strategy, list at least one action you will undertake in the next 12 months. The action should be measurable, time-bound and allocated to a person or group of people within your business.

Financial projections

This is the part that many prospective business owners find the most difficult. However, do persist: setting up a business with no idea of the financial implications can be a recipe for disaster.

Alongside your business plan, prepare a month-by-month budget for the next 12 months, and a cash-flow forecast for the next five years.

Of course, you will need to make a number of assumptions. I recommend that you consider three different scenarios – best case, worst case and expected outcome – so you can see what will happen if things turn out differently from how you imagine.

Again, if you don't have the skills to do these financial projections, get help from someone who does.

Get a grip on tax

One of the main causes of business failure is inability to meet tax obligations. Familiarise yourself with the tax aspects of your business, and make sure you set aside enough money from your business revenue to cover your tax obligations. In New Zealand, these include PAYE ('pay as you earn' income tax), provisional tax, GST (goods and services tax) and FBT (fringe benefit tax), if applicable. The Department of Inland Revenue will provide you with assistance to understand your tax obligations and complete the necessary returns. More information is available at *www.ird.govt.nz*.

Health, safety and working conditions

Health and safety are important considerations. Most New Zealand businesses now require a health and safety system; guidelines can be found at *www.dol.govt.nz*.

If you are going to be employing staff, you also need to be aware of relevant legislation with respect to employment contracts, payment of salaries and wages, holiday pay, overtime, annual leave, sick leave and disciplinary matters. Further information on employment relations for New Zealand businesses can be found at *www.dol.govt.nz*.

Ownership structure

Decide on the ownership structure of your business before you start out. You can choose to be a sole trader, set up a partnership, or set up a company. Each option has different implications in terms of how your income is taxed, and your personal liability if your business gets into financial difficulty.

How to get help

Anyone who sets up a business encounters obstacles, so if you are the kind of person who gives up easily don't bother starting out. To survive, you will need large doses of stickability. You will have to figure out how to get around obstacles, and remain confident in your ability to succeed.

There is plenty of assistance available for new and small businesses, and most of it is free of charge. In New Zealand, the Business in the Community Trust provides a free business mentoring service called Business Mentors New Zealand – you can find details at *www.businessmentor.org.nz*.

New Zealand Trade and Enterprise also offers many support services through Biz Centres located throughout the country. These centres offer helpful free courses.

For more information on business support, check out these websites:

- *www.business.govt.nz* (New Zealand government website for businesses)
- *www.nzte.govt.nz* (New Zealand Trade and Enterprise)
- *www.tsbc.co.nz* (The Small Business Company Limited)
- *www.technz.co.nz* (Technology New Zealand).

8

How to protect your money

IN 'PROTECT YOUR NEST EGG' ON PAGE 189, I DISCUSSED how important it is to protect the wealth that you create. There are many ways to lose your wealth: illness, death, redundancy, relationship breakdown, business failure and other adverse events. Most of these cannot be foreseen, but any of them can seriously set you back.

There are several things you can do to protect your assets and investments, but as you will no doubt realise, the time to act is now, rather than later.

Insurance

A bewildering number of different types of insurance are available. Often I have to deal with people who, unfortunately, have thought about insurance only when it's too late.

I recommend to my clients that they think very carefully about all the options, get as much information as they can, and take steps to get cover – now rather than later.

Trauma cover and total, permanent disablement insurance

These policies provide cover for such things as heart attack, cancer and stroke. They provide a lump sum which can be used to:

- provide income while you take time to fully recover
- clear major debts, reducing stress so you can concentrate on recovering
- enable you to take a holiday to help you recover or spend quality time with your family
- pay for extra or alternative medical treatments
- pay for expensive follow-up drug treatments
- make changes to your lifestyle, home or car
- take time to retrain if necessary.

When purchasing this type of insurance, make sure you are clear about which illnesses and disabilities are covered. A low premium may indicate that the cover is limited to a few illnesses.

With total and permanent disablement, be sure to check how this is defined. Ideally, you should have cover that applies when you are no longer able to do the job for which you are trained, as opposed to unable to work at any occupation whatsoever.

Life insurance

Life insurance is a lump sum that is paid on death or, in some cases, when you are diagnosed with a terminal illness. How would your family cope without you? If there are people who are dependent on you or your income for their financial security, or if you have large debts such as a mortgage, the people you leave behind may suffer ongoing hardship without you.

Life cover provides a lump sum to your family to cover:

- lost income – either short-term or long-term
- bereavement costs, such as funeral and legal fees
- child-raising costs and education
- mortgage repayment to secure the family home
- outstanding debt, such as credit card, hire-purchase and personal loans
- retirement savings lost through the death of the contributor.

If you have a family trust, consider placing the ownership of your life insurance with it. This way, should you die the policy will not be caught up in your estate, which could take some time to settle. Instead, your trust beneficiaries will have immediate access to it to pay funeral expenses and bills.

Life insurance is a handy way of dealing with your beneficiaries if you enter a second relationship. If you have a new partner and wish him or her to have the use of your family home and other assets after your death, you can purchase *two* life insurance policies – one for the benefit of your partner and one for the benefit of your children. This will provide an immediate inheritance for your children on your death, rather than leaving them to wait until your new partner dies, a state of affairs that can cause considerable ill-feeling.

There are four types of life insurance – term life cover, endowment policies, whole-of-life cover and investment linked policies. With all except term life cover, the insurance cover is combined with savings and investment.

Term life insurance

Term life is the simplest form of cover, and the premiums are low because you are paying only for insurance: there is no savings element. However, this also means that the policy has no value. Insuring your life with term cover is similar to insuring your house – if you don't make a claim, you get nothing back.

Endowment policies

Endowment policies are a combination of insurance and investment – with the emphasis on investment. At a fixed maturity date, you receive a lump sum payment. Should you die before then, your beneficiaries receive the insured value of the policy.

Endowment policies are sometimes used to save for specific long-term purposes, such as children's educational fees or retirement. They have a 'surrender' or 'cash' value, but if you cash them up before maturity you lose bonuses. If you have had an endowment policy for some time, this loss of bonuses can be significant.

An alternative to surrendering an endowment policy is to leave it in force but sell it to an investor or family member. Your life would still be the life insured, but the purchaser would pay the premiums and receive the proceeds when you die, or when the policy matures. Selling it rather than surrendering it means the bonuses stay intact and you will receive more money for it. In New Zealand, the Life Insurance Policy Exchange can arrange for the sale of your endowment policy to an investor, providing the policy meets certain conditions. Further information on this can be obtained from *www.policyexchange.co.nz*.

Whole-of-life policies

Whole-of-life policies combine insurance and investment, but these two components are not identified separately, which makes it difficult to see how the savings and investment elements are performing. These days, it is more common for insurance to be sold separately from savings and investment so it is clear how much of your monthly contribution is going into each category, and what your return is.

Whole-of-life policies have a 'surrender' or 'cash' value, but this will be less than the value if you hold the policy to maturity. If you have owned it for some time, it may not be worthwhile surrendering it. It can be useful to retain an old whole-of-life policy with a low insured value to cover funeral expenses.

Investment-linked policies

Investment-linked policies are similar to whole-of-life policies, except that they try to show how much of your monthly contribution goes to insurance and how much to savings and investment. They are usually old-style products that are no longer open to new business, and often costly as well as complex.

If you have an investment-linked policy, I urge you to review its cost structure and performance, particularly it this is your only savings. You may find it is more cost-effective to replace it with term life cover and set up a separate savings scheme. There may be significant penalties if you cash it up – either a loss of bonus or a withdrawal penalty – so you will have to weigh this up against the benefits of replacing it.

Income-protection insurance

Your biggest financial asset is your future income. Most of us will earn between one and two million dollars in our lifetimes, and the loss of this income can have disastrous effects. The worst-case scenario is being so chronically ill or disabled you can no longer work. Not only will you not produce an income, your family will be faced with the burden of paying considerable medical and other bills to keep you alive.

Income-protection insurance is therefore well worth considering, as it will enable you to maintain your lifestyle in the case of long-term illness or disability. This form of insurance will give you income to pay:

- your mortgage payments
- food bills
- living expenses
- educational and other opportunities for your children.

Some people choose to rely on sick leave, but a serious illness may last longer than the leave you have available. In New Zealand, the Accident Compensation Corporation (ACC) will provide replacement income, but this covers only accidents, not illness. And relying on a partner's income to tide you over is not wise: your partner may have to reduce his or her work hours to take care of you and the children.

You can reduce the cost of income-protection insurance by:

- increasing the stand-down period between the onset of illness and the payment of the insurance benefit
- purchasing trauma cover to provide replacement income during the stand-down period
- choosing to have the benefit paid for a shorter than usual period – the maximum period is up to the age of 65.

Hospital and specialist cover

Around 15 percent of adults are admitted to hospital every year. In the West, the average age of the population is increasing so there is ever more pressure on the health system. Government funding has not been able to keep up with the increased demand for health services, and operations such as hip replacements and cataracts, which are considered to be non-urgent, may be given low priority. As a result more people are having to pay for treatment costs themselves or rely on private medical insurance.

By taking out medical insurance, you have the option of choosing private health care to avoid long waiting lists. This cover can be extended to include specialists and X-ray fees, which can be expensive if the illness is long-lived.

The longer you wait before taking out medical insurance, the more likely it is that you will develop a condition that may be excluded from your cover or add to your premiums, so it is best to attend to it while you are still young and healthy.

Family trusts

Another way of protecting the wealth you create is to set up a family trust. A family trust is a legal way to protect and hold assets for your family and should be set up with the help of a solicitor.

There are costs involved in establishing and maintaining a trust and these need to be weighed up against the benefits. A trust needs to be administered properly. There should be records kept of what the trust owns, records of meetings of trustees, and income tax returns prepared for the trust if it owns income-producing assets.

There are three key parties to a trust.

The settlor – the person who establishes the trust.

The trustees – the people responsible for its operation in accordance with the trust deed.

The beneficiaries – the people who benefit from the trust.

It is common for the person establishing the trust – the settlor – to be a trustee. He or she can also be a beneficiary.

Trusts have their own ownership and tax status. Assets are transferred to the ownership of the trust, and a debt is created from the trust back to the settlor. The trustees then decide how best to manage the assets for the beneficiaries.

You can gain one or more of these benefits from transferring assets to the ownership of a trust:

Reduced income tax

Income from assets owned by a trust can either be taxed as trust income, or passed through to the beneficiaries (for example, your spouse or partner, and children over the age of 16) and taxed at their tax rate. This can result in considerable tax savings.

Creditor protection

The use of trusts for this purpose is growing. Many people in business and the professions are increasingly aware of personal liabilities that may attach to them. For example, a company director may be sued for negligence, or a partner in a legal or accountancy firm be responsible for work-related debts of fellow partners. There is a considerable benefit in protecting your lifestyle and putting some investment assets beyond the reach of potential creditors through transferring them to a family trust.

Rest-home subsidy protection

You can qualify for a government rest-home subsidy only if you have a modest level of assets. By transferring assets to a trust, a person may qualify for a subsidy when they wouldn't otherwise. However, this needs to be regarded as an *added* benefit, not the sole benefit, as a trust may not protect your assets if its sole purpose is deemed to be eligibility for rest-home subsidies.

Asset protection for children and grandchildren

A trust can have a life span of up to 80 years, and can therefore protect assets not only for individuals, but for their children and grandchildren.

Relationship property claims or creditor claims

If benefits payable to children or grandchildren are kept within a trust, creditors of these beneficiaries cannot make a claim and the beneficiaries' inheritances will be protected. Similar protections apply in relation to the Property (Relationships) Act. If an inheritance becomes mingled with the beneficiary's relationship property, such as money used to purchase a home, the inheritance can be treated as relationship property. A trust can be useful in reducing this risk.

Dealing with irresponsible or intellectually impaired children and grandchildren

Most individuals can't plan the time of their death, and therefore assets may pass to beneficiaries at an inappropriate time. By having assets in a trust, you allow the trustees to use their discretion as to when to make them available to the beneficiaries – namely when they consider the beneficiaries to be sufficiently mature and responsible. Intellectually impaired children may need to have their affairs managed within a trust throughout their lifetime.

Protection against future means tests, capital gains tax and death duty

Trusts can be sufficiently flexible and structured in such a broad way that there is every prospect they will provide protection against future taxes or means tests that may relate to government benefits.

Easier administration of your estate

If most of your assets are owned by a trust, and your personal assets are few and low in value, when you die your estate administration will be very straightforward, with considerable savings in time and cost.

Should you set up a family trust?

A trust can be of benefit in these circumstances.

- You have recently begun or changed a relationship, through marriage, separation, divorce or widowhood.
- You have a dependant with special needs – for example, a physically or intellectually disabled child.
- You own your business or are a company director.
- You are in a profession (for example, law, consultancy or engineering) where you may be sued.
- You wish to protect your children's inheritance from their present or future partner.
- You have more than one family to consider.

It is best to consult an expert in family trusts to discuss whether one would be useful for you.

How to set up a family trust

1. The settlor decides on the terms of the family trust, including who the trustees and beneficiaries will be, and has a trust deed prepared.

2. The settlor and trustees sign the trust deed.

3. The settlor selects the assets that are to be transferred to the trust, usually the family home and any major investments.

4. A deed records the sale of the assets from the settlor to the trust.

5. The assets are transferred to the trust, and the trust acknowledges (by a deed of acknowledgement of debt) that it owes the settlor an amount equal to the purchase price of these assets.

6. Depending on circumstances, the settlor can then begin a programme of reducing the amount the trustees owe. This is done by annual gifts (by a deed of forgiveness from the settler to the trust) of up to $27,000 if the gifts are to be free of gift duty, or more if there is some urgency to remove the loan from the settlor's personal assets.

If you are intending to set up a trust, do it as soon as possible. The longer you wait, the more your assets will grow in value and the longer your gifting programme may take.

The assets must have been fully gifted for some years (usually at least five) before they are fully protected from asset-testing and creditors.

How to manage your family trust

For a trust to be upheld it must be properly administered. A trust is a separate legal identity and must be treated as such. Trust assets cannot be treated as if they are the personal property of the settlor or settlors, or the trust will be deemed a sham and you will lose the benefits of having it.

To help create an arm's length relationship between personal assets and trust assets, it is useful, although not essential, to have an independent trustee, whose approval is required for all major decisions on trust assets. Trustee companies take on the role of independent trustee in a professional capacity, as do some solicitors and accountants. Be warned though, that if you appoint an independent trustee but don't involve them in trust affairs, your actions may backfire as it will become even more obvious that you are treating trust assets as if they are your own.

There is considerable liability associated with being a trustee, as beneficiaries can take legal action against trustees if the trust assets are not managed prudently. It is, therefore, becoming increasingly difficult to find people other than professional trustees who are willing to take on the role of independent trustee. Involving friends or family members can have disadvantages, as you need to fully disclose your financial affairs to that person and involve them in your decision-making. This means a loss of privacy, and potential conflict.

If your trust owns assets other than just your family home, it should have its own bank account and IRD number. You must keep proper accounting records, including:

- a balance sheet showing trust assets and liabilities, and
- an income tax return.

You will need to:

- arrange for the annual gifting to be done, and
- take note of any distribution of income and capital to the trust beneficiaries.

The trustees should meet at least once a year and prepare a set of minutes for that meeting. Meetings should also be held when major decisions are required, and the decisions minuted. You may want to employ the services of a trustee company to do this administration for you for a fee if you are unsure of what to do, or don't want the administrative burden.

Asset-splitting and testamentary trusts

If you want to avoid the hassle and cost of setting up a family trust, another option is to set up a testamentary trust, which will come into operation on your death. A testamentary trust is simply a trust that is created through your will. You retain ownership and control of your assets until you die, and then they are transferred to your trust without incurring gift duty.

A testamentary trust can be combined quite effectively with asset-splitting to help reduce the size of your estate – that is, the amount of property you own personally when you die – while still allowing your beneficiaries to access the benefits of all the wealth you have created.

CASE STUDY

You and your partner jointly own a house worth $500,000 and investments worth $100,000. Joint ownership means that if one of you dies the ownership of the asset will transfer, as of right, to the other.

You can, however, set up a trust that will give the surviving partner the benefits of the assets without owning them, therefore giving future protection from asset-testing or income-testing of benefits or estate duty.

Here's how. Change the ownership of your house from joint ownership to tenants in common, and divide the investments into two equal portfolios, one owned by each of you.

On the death of one partner, the half-share of the house he or she owns will transfer not to the surviving partner but in accordance with the provisions of the will.

If the will provides for the establishment of a testamentary trust, with the surviving partner included as a beneficiary, this person will have access (at the discretion of the trustees) to the benefits of the trust assets – a half-share in the house and a $50,000 investment portfolio – but without being the owner of the assets.

CASE STUDY **TESTAMENTARY TRUST**

8

Choosing and working with a financial adviser

WHILE IT'S GREAT TO TAKE RESPONSIBILITY FOR YOUR own financial affairs, it is helpful to have input from an expert who is involved full-time in advising clients how best to manage their money. You may decide you need some substantial advice, or maybe you just need someone to run some ideas past. Financial advisers can offer you as much or as little help as you need. The most important thing is to find an adviser whom you trust and feel comfortable with.

Finding a good adviser

Talk to three or so different advisers before you select one, making sure you obtain estimates of their fees for the sort of advice you want.

When you are considering using the services of a particular adviser, set up an initial meeting. You should not expect to pay anything for this meeting if the purpose is solely to establish whether or not you will use the person's services.

At this meeting, you should request a copy of the adviser's disclosure document. This will set out certain information about how the adviser conducts their business, and their qualifications and experience.

There are 16 questions I recommend you ask at this first meeting. Take this list with you.

1. Which organisation do you work for?
2. What are your qualifications and experience?
3. Are you a member of a professional body? If so, which one?
4. Is the organisation for which you work owned, either in full or in part, by another organisation whose investments you may recommend to me?
5. Do you or the organisation have any ties with product or service suppliers? If so, are you tied to one supplier or a range of suppliers?
6. What is the range of services you offer?
7. Is there any area of finance on which you are not qualified to advise me?
8. Do you provide written advice?
9. How are you paid?
10. Will you be paid a commission for investments that you organise for me, and if so will you disclose in advance what that commission is?

11 Will you give me an estimate of the cost of providing advice before you commence working for me?

12 What sources of information and research do you use?

13 How do you stay up-to-date with developments in the market?

14 Do you have professional indemnity insurance? What is the amount of cover?

15 Can you supply a list of referees?

16 To whom can I complain if I am unhappy with the advice you give me?

Many of the answers to these questions should be in the disclosure document given to you by the adviser.

What service will be provided?

Once you have chosen an adviser, here's what you can expect.

- The adviser will ask you to complete a comprehensive questionnaire. This will cover your personal details, present financial situation, and goals. Such information is needed for the adviser to give you good advice.
- The adviser should provide you with advice in writing, with clear reasons and evidence for the advice given.
- The written advice should specify any future costs involved with implementation of the advice. These may be upfront costs, ongoing costs, or a mixture of the two.
- Your adviser should keep in regular contact with you and respond to all queries.
- If your adviser is managing your investment portfolio, you should receive regular quarterly or half-yearly reports, and these should be informative and easy to understand.

It is important that you disclose all relevant information to your adviser, and, if the service is ongoing, keep him or her informed of any changes in your circumstances. If there is information you don't want to disclose, you should let the adviser know this, but bear in mind that it may affect the quality of the advice given to you.

If you don't understand or feel comfortable with the advice you are given, don't act on it. Your adviser may not have fully understood your needs, or have given you insufficient information or explanation. If the advice seems complicated when you were looking for a simple solution, tell your adviser how you feel.

At the end of the day your financial affairs are your responsibility, and you yourself must make the final decision, based on the information presented.

Don't ever delegate responsibility for your financial affairs entirely to another person.

Further reading

Books

The 9 Steps to Financial Freedom: Practical and spiritual steps so you can stop worrying, Suze Orman: Three Rivers Press, 1997

Borrowing to Invest: The fast way to wealth?, Noel Whittaker and Paul Resnik: Simon & Schuster Australia, 2002

The Breakthrough Experience: A revolutionary new approach to personal transformation, John Demartini: Hay House, 2002

Building Wealth through Investment Property, Jan Somers and Dolf de Roos: de Roos Associates Ltd, 1995

The Complete Guide to Residential Property Investment in New Zealand, Andrew King and Lisa Dudson: Random House, 2003

Family Trusts: A New Zealand guide, Martin Hawes: Shoal Bay Press, 1995

For Richer For Poorer: A plain English guide to help sensible Kiwis get real about relationships, money and the law, Maria Konings and Deborah Hollings: CCH, 2001

How To Make One Hell of a Profit and Still Get to Heaven, John Demartini: Hay House, 2004

Landlording in New Zealand: A complete manual for rental property owners, 2nd edition, Frank Saxton: F. L. Saxton & Associates, 1996

The Millionaire Next Door: The surprising secrets of America's wealthy, Thomas J. Stanley and William D. Danko: Longstreet Press, 1996

New Zealand Real Estate Investors' Secrets: How 10 New Zealanders became millionaires from residential property and how you can too! Graeme Fowler: Cliff Press, 2003

Property Investment in New Zealand: A strategy for wealth, Martin Hawes: Shoal Bay Press, 1996

Ready Set Goal! Choose your goals, stay motivated, attract success, Wendy Buckingham: Prentice Hall, 2002

The Richest Man in Babylon, George S. Clason: Penguin Books, 1991

Rich Dad Poor Dad: What the rich teach their kids about money that the poor and middle class do not!, Robert T. Kiyosaki: TechPress, 1997

The Science of Getting Rich, Wallace D. Wattles: Destiny Books, 1976

The Secret, Rhonda Byrne: Atria Books, 2006

Smart Couples Finish Rich: 9 steps to creating a rich future for you and your partner, David Bach: Broadway Books, 2001

Smart Women, Smart Money: Live the life you want, Joan Baker: Allen & Unwin, 2004

The Joy of Not Working: Ernie Zalinski: Ten Speed Press, 2003

The Success Principles: How to get from where you are to where you want to be, Jack Canfield and Janet Switzer: HarperCollins 2007

Think and Grow Rich, Napoleon Hill: Aventine Press, 2005

The Woman's Money Book: It's your money – why not make the most of it?, Vivienne James: Allen & Unwin, 2003

You Don't Make a Big Leap without a Gulp: Finding the courage to change careers and live again, Nigel Beckford and Michael Fitzsimons: FitzBeck Publishing, 2005

Websites

Business

www.business.govt.nz New Zealand government website for businesses

www.nzte.govt.nz New Zealand Trade and Enterprise

www.tsbc.co.nz The Small Business Company Limited

www.technz.co.nz Technology New Zealand for business

Financial advice

www.moneymaxcoach.com Moneymax coaching

www.sorted.org.nz Retirement Commission

Investing

www.goodreturns.co.nz Online money management magazine

www.sharechat.co.nz Forum for share investors

www.interest.co.nz Online interest rates

www.nzx.com New Zealand Stock Exchange

www.asx.com.au Australian Stock Exchange

www.finance.yahoo.com Financial information

www.smartmoney.com Online financial magazine

www.standardandpoors.co.nz Credit rating agency

www.kiwisaver.govt.nz Inland Revenue information on KiwiSaver

www.looklearninvest.org.nz New Zealand Securities Commission

Property

www.dbh.govt.nz Department of Building and Housing (Tenancy Services)

www.qv.co.nz Quotable Value New Zealand

www.qvinsider.co.nz Quotable Value New Zealand property investment information service

www.nzpif.org.nz New Zealand Property Investors' Federation

www.terranet.co.nz Terralink property information

www.reinz.co.nz Real Estate Institute of New Zealand

www.propertytalk.com Online magazine and chat room

Index

achiever 14, 17
  asset allocation 168
  case study 18, 53
  changing behaviour 54, 57–58
  cost-cutting 124
  debt 152, 157
  desires of the 48
  increasing income tips 85, 133
  investments 161, 167, 179, 182, 233
  leveraging 176
  money management 135
  motivation 31, 48
  needs 89
  relationships 65–71
    with entrepreneur 70
    with hoarder 67–68
    with thrill-seeker 69
  respect for money 31
  risk protection 198–200
  risk-taking 161
  saving 113
  stage of life 41
  wealth creation 85, 186–87, 202
  wealth protection 199
  windfall 213
addiction, *see* spending addiction
adviser, *see* financial adviser
asset allocation 168–72, 177–78
  case study 170, 171
assets 77–83, 158, 195, 244, 261–73
asset-splitting trusts 272

bank accounts 136–37, 143–44, 209, 271
bank deposits 158
beliefs about money 24–29
  case study 26, 28
bonds 131, 158, 159
  corporate bonds 220, 234–36
borrowing, capacity 176
  to invest 172
budgeting 117
  see also Federation of Family Budgeting Services
business 250–59
  case study 252
  investment in 220
  franchising 253
  networking (case study) 49
  ownership 164
  partnership 132
  plan 255–57

calculator, KiwiSaver 228
  living expenses 145
  mortgage repayment 156
  property returns 242
  retirement 105
  savings 97
capital gains 130, 182
capital notes 220, 234–36
case study
  achiever 4–5
  asset allocation 170, 171
  beliefs about money 26, 28

business ownership 252
debt trap 121
entrepreneur 20, 66
financial experiences 47
hoarder 4–5, 16, 53, 66
motivation 49
perception of wealth 42, 44
retirement capital 101
retirement savings plan 104
role of money 90–91
thrill-seeker 22, 59
total money-management system 147
cash management fund 158
children, endowment policies 264
planning for education (case study) 91
reassessing finances for 214
company, credit rating 162
limited liability 132
Loss Attributing Qualifying 244–45
compound interest 97, 116
corporate bonds 220, 234–36
cost-cutting tips 124–25
Court for Summary Instalment Order 122
credit card 118–19
credit crisis (2007) 162
creditor protection 267–68

debt 118–25
short term 151–52
debt trap 120–22
case study 121
de facto couples 194, 197
death of partner 211
dependants (case study) 91
see also children
Depression, the 1930s 29
direct investments 220, 233–59
discretionary expenditure 84–85
divorce 211–12
see also relationships

education, children's (case study) 91
emergency funds 94–95, 152–53, 189–90
employment *see* job
endowment policies 131, 264
enduring power of attorney 195–97
entrepreneur 14, 19–20
asset allocation 168–69
business ownership 250
case study 20, 66
changing behaviour 55–58
cost-cutting 124
debts 120, 152
desires of the 48
increasing income tips 133
investment 166, 179, 233
money-management 135
motivation 48
needs 89
property investment 233
relationships 65–71
with achiever 70
with hoarder 88, (case study) 66
with thrill-seeker 70
respect for money 32
risk protection 189, 198, 200
risk-taking 161
saving 113
shareholding 233
as a speculator 182
stage of life 41
wealth creation 85, 187–88, 202
wealth protection 199
windfall 213
equity funds 130
estate planning 131–32, 193–97, 215
expenditure 84–85, 117
expenses 137, 141–45, 148

family trusts 132, 189, 244, 267–72
Federation of Family Budgeting Services 122
finance company debentures 158, 220, 234–35
financial adviser 275–78
financial assets 76–83
financial experiences 45–47
case study 47
fixed expenditure 84
fixed-interest investments 158, 220
franchising, business 253
Friedman's Type A/B theory 13
fund management 220
gift duty 131–32

goal setting 90, 93–109
golden rules, for setting up a money-management system 149
  for increasing net worth 79
growth assets 158
growth portfolio 169

health insurance 215
hoarder 14–16
  asset allocation 168
  case study 4–5, 16, 53, 66
  changing behaviour 52–53, 57–58
  cost-cutting 124
  debts 152
  financial experiences 45
  increasing income tips 133
  investment 166, 179, 182, 233
  leveraging 176
  money management 135
  motivation 48
  needs 89
  relationships 65–71
    with achiever 67–68
    with entrepreneur 68, (case study) 66
    with thrill-seeker 68–69
  respect for money 30–31
  risk protection 198–99
  risk-taking 161
  saving 112
  stage of life 41
  wealth creation 85, 185–86, 202
  wealth protection 200
  windfall 213
home equity release 183–84

income, increasing (case study) 129
  passive 128
  protection insurance 215, 265–66
  tips for increasing 133
inheritance 212–13
insurance 189–93, 215, 262–66
  hospital and specialist 266
  income protection 265–66
  life 265
  trauma and permanent disablement 262
interest, compound 97, 116
  credit card 119
  expenses and 131
  on home equity mortgage 184
  mortgage 119
  reducing interest paid 118–24
investment 130–31, 220–33
  borrowing for 172–76
  in business 220
  capital notes 220
  corporate bonds 220
  direct investments 220, 233–59
  endowment policies 264
  finance company debentures 220, 234–35
  with finance company 235
  fixed-interest 220, 234
  insurance 265
  PIE *see* Portfolio Investment Entities
  portfolio 157–60, 164–65, 177–79
  Portfolio Investment Entities 222, *see also* superannuation schemes
  in property 46, 220, 237–50
  risk protection 161–67, 261–73
  in shares 180, 220, 233–34, *see also* shares
investment assets 77

job, finding a new, *see* increasing income
  loss 213
  self-employment 132

KiwiSaver 107, 130, 150, 152, 227–30

LAQC *see* Loss Attributing Qualifying Company
leaky bucket syndrome 116
leveraging 172–76, 180
life goals 95–96
life insurance 190–93, 265
Life Insurance Policy Exchange 264
limited liability companies 132–33
line of credit 153
listed trusts 230–31
living expenses 141–45
Loss Attributing Qualifying Company 244–45

managed funds 220–33
margin lending 174
marginal tax 132, 151
money-management system, *see* total money-management system
mortgage, interest 119
  paying off 156
  repayment penalty costs 152
  in share portfolio 174
  structure 245–46
motivation 48–49
  case study 49
Myers-Briggs Type Indicator 13

networking *see* business networking

ordinary power of attorney 196–97

passive income 128
perception of wealth 42–45
  case study 42, 44
permanent disablement insurance 262
personality *see* achiever, entrepreneur, hoarder, thrill-seeker
PIE *see* Portfolio Investment Entities
plan, business 255–57
  retirement savings 97–106
  savings 107–108
Portfolio Investment Entities 222–23
  see also superannuation schemes
power of attorney 189, 195–97
property, assets 80–81
  buying first house 153–56
  calculating return 240
  investment 46, 164–65, 220, 237–50, 247
  managed property funds 249–50
  ownership 244
  portfolio 239, 248–50
  tax 131–33
  tenancy law 246
  trusts 249–50
Property (Relationships) Act 132, 138, 189, 197–98, 214–15

relationships, between money personalities 65–71
  case studies 4–5, 47
  de facto couples 194, 197
  death of partner 211
  divorce 211
  estate planning 131–32, 193–97, 215
  money management 137–49
  property in 131–33, *see also* Property (Relationships) Act
  separation 211
  tax minimisation 131–33
Residential Tenancies Act 246
retirement, asset allocation (case study) 171
  calculator 105
  capital, calculating 100–106
  case study 101, 104
  endowment policies 264
  goal setting for 95, 97–109
  income, calculating 99
  KiwiSaver 107, 130, 150, 152, 227–30
  Portfolio Investment Entities 222–23
  property 80–81, 104, 249–50
  rest-home subsidy protection 268
  savings, calculating 102–106
  superannuation schemes 150, 152, 220, 225–26
  transition into 215–16
risk and return 160–61
risk, reducing 161–67, 189–200, 261–73
role of money 88–92
  case study 90–91

saving 112–25
  compound interest 97
  Equation, the Savings 114
  and investment portfolio 157–64
  leaky bucket syndrome 116
  long term 158
  for medium term spending 157–58
  planner 108
  for retirement 102–104
  risk protection 189
  tax minimisation 130
  tips for 115
Savings Equation, the 114
self-employed 132
self-insurance 191

separation 211
  see also relationships
shares 130, 159–60, 180–81, 220, 233–34
  company structure 132
  mortgaging to buy 174
  risk and return 160, 164
sole trader 132
spending, addiction 33
  assets 81
  budgeting 117
    see also Federation of Family Budgeting Services
stages in life 34–41
Standard and Poor's rating system 162–63
superannuation 150, 152, 220, 225–26
    see also KiwiSaver *and* Portfolio Investment Entities

tax 130–33, 245–46
  capital gains 182
  marginal tax rate 151
  property investment 240
  trusts 267
tenancy law 246
term life insurance 264
testamentary trusts 195, 272–73
thrill-seeker 14, 21–22
  asset allocation 168–69
  case study 22, 59
  changing behaviour 56–59
  cost-cutting 124
  debt 120, 152, 157
  increasing income tips 133
  investment 166, 182, 233
  leveraging 176
  managing investment portfolio 179
  money management 135
  motivation 48
  needs 90
  property 233
  relationships 65–71
    with achiever 69
    with entrepreneur 70
    with hoarder 68–69
  respect for money 32–33
  risk protection 189, 198, 200
  risk-taking 161
  saving 112
  shareholding 161, 233
  wealth creation 85, 188, 202
  wealth protection 200
  windfall 213
tips, cutting costs 124–25
  increasing income 85, 133
  investing 166–67
  making the most of your money personality 52–57
  saving 115
  wealth-protection 199–201
total disablement insurance 262
total money-management system 134–49
  case study 147
trauma cover 262
trust, asset-splitting and testamentary 195, 272–73
  family 132, 195, 244–45, 267–72
  listed 220, 230–31
  power of attorney 195–97
  property 249–50

wealth creation, assets and 76–83
  influences on 75, 167
  perceptions 43
  planning 203–206, 217
  protection 189, 200
  strategies 185
  see also achiever, entrepreneur, hoarder, thrill-seeker
whole-of-life policies 264–65
wills 189, 193–94, 212
windfall 212–13

Want to know more?

www.moneymaxcoach.com

You've read the book, and now you are ready to put what you have learned into practice. Throughout the book I have shown you the tools that will help you uncover your money personality, and use this knowledge to maximise your money, invest it successfully, protect it wisely, and enjoy life to the full. On my website **www.moneymaxcoach.com** you will find everything you need to create a plan just for you, including calculators, workbooks, audio files and much more. Get started now!

Liz